Life in the Balance

Titles in Harvestime's **Life Choices** series:

Life in the Balance, by Sue Williams

Blind Spot, by Liz Priestley

Over the Edge, by Audrey Constant

Life in the Balance

Sue Williams

Harvestime

Published in the United Kingdom by:
Harvestime Publishing Ltd, 69 Main Street, Markfield
Leicester LE6 0UT

First published by Harvestime
First printed February 1992

British Library Cataloguing in Publication Data
A catalogue record for this book
is available from the British Library

ISBN 1-872877-09-5

Typeset in the United Kingdom by:
ScribeTech Ltd, Bradford BD8 7BX
Printed and bound in the United Kingdom by:
Richard Clay Ltd, Bungay, Suffolk

Contents

1

Birthdays and black bean sauce

Saturday

I bought a birthday card for Chloe at Bates' this morning.

I wanted to get the one with William Tell aiming at a kid with an apple on his head – the caption said, 'Missing You'. Because I *do* miss her, very much. But it seemed more the kind of thing a boyfriend should send, and, anyway, it wasn't birthdayish.

In the end I chose the one with a fish on it. But it doesn't feel appropriate somehow. None of them did. And now I've got it home, I'm just sitting, staring at it, because it's stirring up too many memories.

I still feel so churned up inside about what happened that sometimes I don't know what to do with myself. When I look back, it seems unbelievable that Clo's birthday this time last year could have been so . . . so *normal*.

Maybe it's just as well that you can't predict the future. I mean, if I'd known then, I'd have *emigrated* – I honestly would.

Which is stupid really, because – whichever way you look at it – this is Chloe's story. The problem's Chloe's, not mine. Or is it? . . .

* * *

Chloe's birthday is in September, and last year it was on a Friday. We were labelling diagrams of the alimentary canal in biology when she suddenly whispered, 'You know, now I'm sixteen, I *can*!' As if it had only just struck her.

'Shut up, you idiot!' said Tamsin. 'Wiggie'll hear you. Anyway – can what?'

'*You* know!' Chloe hissed, pinkly – because it wasn't the kind of thing she usually talked about. 'When you're sixteen, you're *allowed* to. Aren't you?'

Well, *were* you allowed to? This was one of life's great imponderables. In the meantime, though, Wiggie's X-ray ears were homing in on our conversation. We took evasive action, and by the time his gaze swept around to our bench we were totally absorbed in salivary amylase.

But I could tell this was likely to develop into one of our intense breaktime debates – Could you? Should you? and Would you? If not, why not? And if so, when?

Which was all totally theoretical, I mused, chewing my Biro. None of us had a boyfriend or any current prospect of one. And the boys in our class were such an uninspiring collection that no sane female could ever fancy them – no matter *what* Jane Soper says.

But the sixth form – now *there* was a hotbed of talent for you.

I glanced at Chloe curiously; perhaps she *did* like someone after all. Which would have been an interesting development, as up to now I'd always thought of her as career-minded, not boy-minded like the rest of us. She knew where she was going in life – graphic design – and how she was going to get there – college.

That was one of the big differences between us, and I really respected her for it. Not that I'd ever tell her that, of course. We lived about ten minutes' walk away from each other, Chloe and me, and we'd been friends ever since Miss Cooke sat us at the same tiny desk at infants' school.

We used to spend a lot of time together, partly because Clo's mother was a bit, well, *unconventional*, and kept erratic hours. Her dad had faded out of the picture when she was tiny, and she didn't remember him.

We shared a Saturday job at Bates' paper-shop. I did mornings; she did afternoons. And we shared clothes and make-up and our whole lives, really. And babysitting.

* * *

'What's that?' I asked, prodding about dubiously with my fork.

'A bean-sprout . . . I think,' said Chloe, peering at it. 'Either that or a caterpillar.'

As discretion is the better part of valour, I decided to leave it for *her* to eat. Chinese wasn't my favourite, but Chloe liked it, and it was *her* birthday. Ruth and Tony had asked us to sit that night, hence our celebration taking the form of a Vegetarian Special for Two from the Pearl Dragon Takeaway (with Ruth's permission, of course).

We liked it best when the twins were still up. I say 'twins' because everyone thought of them that way, although they weren't really twins at all. They were adopted, and there was a three-month age-gap between them, though you'd never have guessed. Last time, we'd spent the entire evening galloping around the lounge on hands and knees being horses.

'They're so fond of you,' Ruth said. 'You're so good with little children.'

'Only when I'm not related to them!' I replied flippantly – but with hidden feeling.

Chloe simply laughed.

It was just as well the twins were asleep tonight, though. I mean, Mushroom Foo Yung can't be *that* easy to scrape off the wallpaper.

I liked the atmosphere at Ruth and Tony's, even though it *did* look like something out of a designer catalogue. It was neutral territory for us, somewhere we could talk. Which we used to do for hours and hours; Chloe always had the most original views on life.

'And on music,' I thought, pushing the Chow Mein in Oyster Sauce around my plate in time to *In the Mood*.

Clo's heart-throbs weren't like anyone else's. Musically, she was into Glenn Miller and cinematically, Humphrey Bogart. She also liked classical music – it helped her paint, she said. She's the only person I've ever met who had a picture of Debussy on her bedroom wall.

'Clo, you're weird!' I said to her once. 'You only like dead people.'

'What's weird about that?' she countered. 'It only proves I've got better taste than you.'

Touché.

I helped myself to some more fried rice.

'Yazz was on top form today, wasn't she?' said Chloe, sucking her fingers.

'Mmm . . .' I agreed. 'She's mad – definitely mad. But you've got to admire her nerve.'

'*I* don't think she's mad,' said Clo, looking straight at me, her eyes wide open. 'I think she's quite right.'

'Oh, come on, Clo. She's a fanatic!' I protested. I liked Yasmin – we all did – but her family were very religious and we'd learnt the hard way that there were some subjects you just *didn't* bring up with her. Which is why lunchtime had turned out so riveting.

It had been raining, so for lack of anything better to do, a gang of us had slipped into the lecture theatre where the debating society was meeting. Trusting souls that we were. We'd *never* have gone in with Yazz if we'd known what the debate was about.

I was whispering something to Cassie when I noticed that Yazz was getting agitated.

'What's the debate?' I asked.

'What's the debate?' Cass hissed at the boy in front.

' "Marriage is an outmoded institution," ' he told her.

'Oh, no!' I said. 'Let's get out of here.'

'. . . safeguard the rights of children and single-parent families . . .' droned the speaker.

I tugged at Yazz's sleeve.

'Come on!' I whispered.

Yazz glared at me. 'I want to hear this out,' she muttered.

I turned to Chloe, shrugged and gave her my oh-well-I-did-my-best face. We knew what Yazz was thinking. So . . . we might as well relax and enjoy the fireworks. When they came – if they came. And they *did*.

'. . . and the only reasonable solution is free love,' a very personable sixth-former was saying.

When you looked at him, you felt he could be right. In fact, definitely.

Then Yasmin stood up, eyes blazing; if looks could kill, he'd have been meat. I winced.

'I think it's *disgusting*,' she shouted, 'the way you all carry on. This country is so . . . so *immoral*! I tell you, if this was Iran, you'd all be stoned or have your hands chopped off. You've got no idea about modesty or faithfulness. Rock music is about nothing but sex. Who wants to buy a cow if he can get the milk for free? Allah will judge you.'

There was a stunned silence, then a few titters.

'Is that it?' asked the chairman, nonplussed.

'That's it!' said Yazz, quickly. And then she suddenly reddened up and bolted for the exit.

'What's bitten *her*?' said the boy in front, swivelling around in his seat. 'What is she – repressed or something?'

'No, just religious,' I said, hurrying after her. 'Someone just pressed the wrong button, that's all.'

We caught up with Yazz eventually. She was looking confused and sweaty, and now that we'd found her, nobody knew quite what to say. There was a long, embarrassed pause.

'Magnificent!' said Clo, at last.

'I just want to be on my own – OK?' said Yazz in a tight little voice.

So we made tracks. We didn't collapse in hysterics until she was out of earshot, though – after all, there *are* limits. She *was* our friend.

'I mean,' continued Chloe, picking a few grains of rice off the shag-pile, 'look at it from her point of view. We marry for love in the West, and we have a thirty per cent divorce rate. How can that look logical?'

'Are you saying,' I asked, dumbfounded, 'that you're in favour of arranged marriages?' I was used to Chloe by now, but this I *couldn't* believe.

'No,' she said. 'Is that Vegetable Satay? Do you want

some? No, what I think is that it's better to be single than marry the wrong person. It's just that, for some reason, *everyone* rushes into it.'

'Don't *you* want to get married, then?'

'Well . . . eventually.'

Chloe always had the power to surprise. I could never understand how someone with such a women's-libby mother could be so old-fashioned, so *traditional*. But that was Clo for you.

'I mean,' she said, 'it's got to be the best relationship in the world. But I'm glad Harriet hasn't married any of *her* boyfriends. That's what I meant about the wrong people.'

That I *could* understand. I dug into my side-order of prawn crackers.

'I still think Yazz is a nut, though,' I pursued. 'She might sound very moral, but she thinks everyone should get married at the age of twelve! Now, that's *beyond*.'

I was struck with a fleeting vision of my younger brother, Joshua George, with a wife, mortgage, car and briefcase. Mad, absolutely mad. Absurd. Ridiculous. Indeed, horrific.

Chloe nodded. 'I'll grant you that,' she said. 'But she's right about waiting for marriage. Sex before marriage just can't be right. I'm going to wait.'

She saw my face.

'Seriously,' she added, hooking her hair behind her left ear.

I looked at her; I was in awe of her when she was like this. She had such strong views – she was very *wise*. Me, I didn't know my own mind at all, and it never particularly bothered me. I just drifted along. Miss Shue said Chloe did all my thinking for me, and I suppose it was true, up to a point.

A lock of Chloe's hair had flopped on to her plate, and she was wiping it clean on a piece of kitchen roll. She smiled across at me; there was a smudge of black bean sauce on her nose. She was rather too well-endowed with nose, I always thought, and it made her look horsy.

But her hair was lovely. Long and dark, like mine – which is why Mrs Harris (Eng. Lit.) still used to muddle us up. Only Clo's was full and wavy, whereas mine was lank and greasy and full of split ends. If I had the chance to redesign myself, I'd put a fair bit of Chloe into the blueprint.

I raised my Coke to her.

'Cheers!' I said. 'Many happy returns, and all that.'

She beamed.

'May you have not only a super birthday – what's left of it – but a great year. May your GCSE revision get easier and easier, and may you get your paintings into Le Becq's.'

I stood up. 'Laaa-deee-z and gentlemen,' I announced, 'I propose a toast. I give you . . . Chloe Prentice!'

'Hear, hear!' she giggled, and we clunked our cans together.

* * *

Could it only have been this time last year? Could we *really* have been so casual about things then? We thought we had all the time in the world.

We didn't realise then how fast the next year would go, how quickly September would turn into July, and the long-dreaded exams become past history.

Or how soon both our lives would be devastated by the chain reaction to one stupid little mistake.

2

Tactical planning

'Shall I wear this . . . or *this*?' Chloe demanded, whirling around with an assortment of skirts and tops pressed against her.

'The blue's nice,' I suggested. 'You look nice in blue.'

'Ye-e-es, but I haven't got the right shoes,' she muttered, dumping the clothes on the bed and scrabbling around underneath to eventually produce, with a 'Ta-da!' a pair of scuffed navy courts.

'Brilliant! I thought I'd sent these to the Refuge,' she said. 'They'll polish up nicely. So how would this look?'

And how she looked was great. She always did. Chloe was like her mum – they just threw on whatever they wanted, and, although sometimes they looked a little *individual*, it was always with style.

As for Chloe's mum – now *there* was an interesting woman for you. An off-the-wall nutter, but nice with it.

Harriet Prentice was the desperately busy type. By day, she was a high-powered secretary in stilettos and Barbie-doll outfit, but off duty she effected a Jekyll & Hyde transformation and went slopping around in dungarees or ethnic floaty stuff as treasurer to some women's pressure group. I couldn't understand how she reconciled the two.

'I work to live; I don't live to work,' she'd pronounce.

Clo said her mum had even turned down a promotion involving extra commitment to the firm because her campaigning was far more important to her. It took up a lot of her evenings, and every now and then she'd be off banning whales or saving bombs or whatever.

Chloe and her mother were very close, more like sisters. Clo used to call her a '*nouveau* hippy'; I called her Mrs P.

'Harriet's got no taste in men at all!' Clo would say. 'She's like a little kid. D'you remember Jeremy?'

A tall, blond, blue-eyed Apollo who'd lasted all of six weeks.

'She thought he was *it*. Do you realise he was living with a guy called Peregrine?'

'No!'

'It's true, I promise you! I could have told her he was gay. But could *she* see it?'

'But – if he was gay – why did he go out with your mum?' I asked, this being out of my league.

'Perry had ditched him, so he did it for revenge. And there she was, congratulating herself on finding an old-fashioned man who wasn't only after one thing. Honestly, Sophie, she's got no idea.'

Mrs P *did* have fascinating boyfriends. ('Not *boyfriends*,' she'd say, 'just *friends*. Although why men seem to think all single women are rampantly lonely and just waiting to ambush the nearest thing in trousers is quite beyond me.')

There had been Ron (a TV producer), Alex (something in politics) and Joe (who was an actor and Almost Famous because he was a supporting cast-member of F*riends and*

Lovers). We used to spend hours poring over the video trying to catch a glimpse of Joe's elbow or the back of his head whenever Twenty-six Bank Road was in shot. He's still in it. And he's still not famous.

I used to envy Chloe her freedom, but she never appreciated it. And it *did* have its down-side. I got very upset when she told me that on Christmas Day last year her mother had gone off on a sit-in outside Number Ten and she'd been left alone all day with nothing to do but watch Noel Edmonds' *Hospital Roadshow*, Wogan's *Bumper Hamper of Fun*, *The Great Escape* and *Fifty Years of the Two Ronnies*. With a cracker.

'I did homework,' she said.

The next time I was over at her house it was as if Mrs P had changed into a different person – I couldn't look at her in the same way.

'You're quiet today, Sophie,' she said.

All I could think was, 'How could she have done that?'

'It was no big deal,' Chloe insisted. 'I just didn't want to go, that's all.'

Perhaps it was tactless to tell Mum about it, but it was one of those things you need to get off your chest to make yourself feel better. Anyway, Mum's great like that; if there's a crisis, she's the first person you want around. She *always* knows what to do, what to say. Not like Harriet Prentice.

'Chloe's welcome here any time; she knows that,' Mum said, putting on that stiff face she uses when she detects a nasty smell or disapproves of something, and she started inviting Clo around more. Sometimes her thoughtfulness embarrasses me.

Chloe liked our house; she said she just liked the family atmosphere. It was something I took for granted when I wasn't hating it – a younger brother and sister can be unbearable, but I shouldn't complain because we *do* at least have separate bedrooms.

But Chloe actually *liked* them. Sometimes when she came for tea she'd spend the whole evening helping Josh make a pressure gauge out of tubes from ball-point pens and bits from Dad's beer-making kit. Or playing My Little Pony with Kate.

'They're sweet!' she'd say. Now, there speaks someone who has never had to get up for school in a five-person-one-bathroom house.

'Chloe, you're out of your tiny mind!' I'd reply. 'They're only pretending to be nice. They're really junior terrorists. Do you know what JG did last week . . . ?'

Chloe might have had poor taste in kids, but she *did* look great in blue. She had tried on her chosen outfit by now, and was pirouetting in front of the mirror. I hadn't decided what I was going to wear tomorrow. In fact, I hadn't decided whether I really wanted to go. And now, I'd give my right arm if it meant we'd stayed home.

'You must!' Chloe insisted. 'All the fifth and sixth'll be there. You can't not go to the end-of-exams disco – you just *can't*.'

Any other time, maybe – but right now my heart wasn't in it. My heart was, in fact, somewhere in the vicinity of Hugh Carter. And Cassie had heard from Karen that he fancied someone else, but they didn't know who.

Hugh was pale and serious in a poetic, romantic kind of way. I hadn't been chasing him – well, not obviously. I'd invested a lot of time hanging around, smiling, wishing, hoping, being nice, being helpful and, most of all, *being there*. But, so far, to no avail.

'Look.' Chloe was ever-practical. 'Hugh's not seeing anyone else – yet. Perhaps you could net him at the disco.'

True. It *could* happen. I could *make* it happen. I brightened.

'Why not?' I said, feeling more positive. 'But what shall I wear?'

Chloe riffled through the hangers and pulled out a striking top in a bronze colour. Not my type of thing at all.

'Go on – try it,' she urged. 'It would look great on you.'

So I tried it on, and it did – perhaps it was the colour.

'And if you put your hair up like this' – Chloe whisked it up into a loose knot – 'and leave it wispy round the sides . . . well, it's brilliant!'

And it was. I looked really elegant. Not like me at all.

'Hugh's bound to notice you like that,' she said. And at that moment I really believed it, too.

'OK, I'll go,' I grinned. 'Now, how about the make-up?'

We pooled our resources and wedged Mrs P's beauty book against the mirror behind a dried-up mug that had once – long, long ago – contained coffee, and attempted to copy a few of the looks. Some were nice; others were, to put it kindly, unflattering.

Things got sillier and sillier. Then, at the back of the drawer, we unearthed an ancient pair of false eyelashes, which inspired the intrepid Miss Prentice. She made me paint a pair of open eyes on her eyelids with highlighter and eye-shadow, applying the lashes as the finishing touch with something called – rather worryingly – 'eyelash cement'.

The end result was quite convincing, if you weren't too close. But it would have been more professional if she hadn't giggled so much.

'You know, if we all did this in class, the teachers would think we were actually awake!' I said.

Chloe snorted. 'Let's try it out on Harriet,' she said.

So I led her carefully down the stairs, and she fumbled

her way into the kitchen, where Mrs P was sitting nursing a teacup across the table from a bearded man.

Chloe's mother shot her a puzzled glance. We just stood there, trying not to laugh and unable to think of a thing to say. That was one of the things I loved about Clo. We had such a lot of *fun* together.

'Are you all right, dear?' asked Mrs P. 'You look a bit peaky.'

'Oh, H*attie!*' Chloe exploded with a huge guffaw, and the penny dropped. It was one of those times when something strikes you as so funny that you can't stop laughing and your cheeks ache and ache but you still can't stop. Eventually we bubbled down, and Mrs P, dabbing at her own mascara, dispensed two mugs of tea. Earl Grey.

'You'd better get those things off before the glue sets,' she said, tinkling the sugar-spoon against the china. 'It's not as easy as it says on the tube.'

'Right you are, boss!' said Chloe with a salute, and she pulled at the lashes as we trailed back upstairs again. One fell off into her tea, where it revolved majestically like a beetle doing breast-stroke, and the other refused to come off at all. It didn't surrender until about ten minutes later, by which time Clo was looking very pink and puffy round the eye.

'Well, I won't try *that* again!' she declared, squinting at herself ruefully in the mirror. She aimed the cement at the bin, and sent it flying in, a perfect arc.

'Well, Howard thought it was funny,' I said.

'That wasn't Howard,' she said flatly. 'That was Barney. We don't talk about Howard.'

The said Howard had made a pass at Chloe one day when her mum was out; I didn't know whether Clo had told her. Howard had had his marching orders long since, anyway. Perhaps Mrs P's chequered love-life was the reason that Chloe was so unimpressed with men in general.

'Romance equals hassle, as far as I can see,' she said. I think also the fact that she was top of the class had something to do with it – how can a boy fancy someone who's brainier than him? But I still wanted her advice about Hugh – she was a valuable ally when it came to planning a campaign.

For instance, I used to like a boy called Ben Vine, and Chloe and I found out where he lived and went for a long and extremely complicated walk to case the joint. I discovered his road and a blister on my heel at approximately the same time, which didn't help matters. Nor did the fact that it was the kind of road that didn't go anywhere.

'You can't just stroll down here,' I protested. 'It's too . . . too *obvious*!'

'Why not? It's a free country,' said Clo, launching out. 'Just act casual.'

Now, I had, of course, visualised Ben as inhabiting a tasteful, artistic house with attractive, interesting parents who would possibly spot me as I walked casually past and invite me in for a sherry or something, whereupon Ben would declare his undying love for me.

Unfortunately, it transpired that this was not particularly likely on Hill Crescent, whose houses looked as if they had taken a collective decision about ten years ago to give up trying. In the hovel stakes, Number Seventy-three was outstanding. Peeling paint, a garden completely neglected and a stripped-down Escort rusting in the drive.

'It's the wrong place,' I said.

'No, it's not – there's his bike,' said Chloe.

'Shut up!' I spluttered, and we carried on walking. Casually.

Now, I know the state of his dad's herbaceous border is no indication of a guy's soul, but it makes you wonder. Exit, therefore, Ben; enter, Hugh.

'How can we find out who he likes?' I asked Chloe, bouncing up and down on her bed. 'I mean, it *could* be me,' though I didn't dare to hope so.

Chloe was philosophical. 'Yasmin might know,' she said. 'Omar sits next to Hugh. We'll all be in tomorrow for careers day – we'll sound her out then.'

'*You* do it, Clo,' I badgered. 'But don't let on I like him, will you?'

Well, it was worth a try. Walking back home later, I drifted off into a fantasy. I replayed it over and over – Hugh asking for a dance, asking me out, kissing me; maybe even *me* asking *Hugh* out. I went over it so many times that I felt I'd covered every angle – I hadn't been a Brownie for nothing, you know. I rehearsed my lines. I was ready. Hugh Carter, watch out . . . .

'Watch out!' someone shrieked, as a football whizzed past my head. I felt the rush of air against my cheek, and I jumped. A good half-metre. I was mortified. Behind me, JG and one of his cronies doubled up with laughter.

'You . . . you *idiot!*' I yelled, feeling hot and cold and shaky and stupid. 'You could have killed me!'

'No way!' JG called back from a safe distance. 'Where there's no sense, there's no feeling.'

'Anyway, it was your fault. You weren't looking where you were going,' said the crony.

'Yeah – you weren't with it. In fact, you were definitely without it!' grinned Joshua George.

'I'm *not* wasting my breath on *them*,' I fumed. Gathering

my shredded self-respect, I walked up our path with as much dignity as I could muster. Which, of course, introduced into the equation a factor I'd overlooked.

When beautiful, poetic, romantic Hugh found out I'd got a brother like JG . . . would he still want to go out with me?

3

Hugh and me, me and Hugh

I was desperate for breaktime next day.

I lost Chloe on the way out of the talk on 'Exciting Accountancy', and when I located her she was already deep in conversation with the others. She was in the process of steering the talk around to the disco, and she shot me a look which meant, 'Hang on – I haven't asked yet.'

I had to admire her expertise. It wouldn't do to appear too obvious – these girls were seasoned veterans, and if they realised I liked Hugh, I'd *never* hear the end of it.

We were getting close now. 'Are you going tonight, Julie?' Clo asked, all innocence.

'No, I can't make it . . . unless I miss my evening class.'

'Well, can't you? Just this once?'

'I don't know,' Julie said, doubtfully. 'I mean, my *parents* enrolled me for it. You don't get a refund if you skip a session.'

The Brays thought Julie was Rembrandt revisited – they used to have Christmas cards printed with her own designs. Wishful thinking, I'd say.

'Anyway,' she added, 'it's the last week of life class.'

'Life class!' squeaked Rosie Blumire. 'You know what life class *is*, don't you?'

'Fruit in bowls?' Cassie volunteered.

'Naked people, that's what!' said Rosie, triumphantly.

Julie went pink.

'Is that *true?*' Tamsin asked.

'Well, yes – but it's not the highlight of my week,' said Julie, trying to look aloof.

'*Men? Starkers?*'

'Altogether,' she said, starting to enjoy the attention.

I groaned inwardly. The conversation was never going to get back on the rails after this.

'And your *folks* enrolled you for this? Do they know what life class is?' Rosie pursued.

'How should I know?' said Ju. 'But, like I said, it's no big deal. Just a few geriatric posers.' Then she brightened. 'Now, it would be different if it was *Bruno* . . .'

'You don't fancy *Bruno*, do you?' said Cassie in astonishment.

Bruno Villebonne was head boy. He was eighteen going on twenty-five, and stood out like a prince against the general tide of gangly spottiness. You could tell just from looking at him that he thought a lot of himself, but you had to admit he had just cause. He was visually *very* rewarding – Latin-looking, hunky, sporty and disconcertingly hairy.

It was even rumoured that he could induce a state of weak-kneedness in Miss Brown (CDT).

And he was famous – Bruno played rugby for the south of England under-twenty-one squad. Fortunately for womankind at large, he had a permanent away fixture with Roo Bartlett, deputy head girl. A pretty intense fixture, by all accounts.

'Bruno may look fantastic, but he's got the brains of a newt,' said Cassie. (Insulting Bruno was a favourite sport of ours.) 'Why, he's so thick he . . . .'

'How come he's got into Oxford, then?' Chloe broke in.

'Because of his biceps, that's why. Everyone knows that. Anyway, what's so great about studying French? Just because his dad brought him up bilingual doesn't mean he can actually *think!*'

Chloe was silenced. So was I. Because the bell was going, Yazz was shouldering her bag and setting off down the corridor. Our beautifully-engineered opportunity to pump her for inside information had gone. Vanished. Sunk without trace.

'Clo, you traitor!' I hissed.

'Calm down, Sophie. I'll ask another time,' she said, a little too quickly, tossing back her long mane and frowning ever so slightly.

'And just what are *you* doing, sticking up for Bruno?' I demanded. 'He's . . . he's an ape!'

'Just cool it,' she said, pushing open the door of Lecture Theatre Two and walking in to the talk on 'Languages – Your Passport to Europe'.

'*Guten Tag, meine Damen und Herren,*' said Mr Cooper.

* * *

It was hard to concentrate. Back in November, having a foreign exchange student had seemed like a good idea, but I was now having trouble remembering why. It suddenly seemed a colossal imposition. We'd just finished our GCSEs – all we wanted was to be left alone. We didn't want careers lectures. Or coach trips. Or students. In fact, we never wanted to see school again.

Madame Launay had called this lunch-time meeting to go through details of next week's agenda, but my mind wasn't on Windsor Castle or Brighton Pavilion. It was on the tennis-courts. Or rather, it wasn't.

Sitting by the window has definite advantages. A few minutes before, I'd noticed Hugh Carter and Gregor Lumb, racquets in hand, heading for the tennis-courts. Which was interesting – *and* aggravating, because only one corner of the court was within my field of vision. And Hugh hadn't leapt into it recently.

He could be anywhere. Still playing. Or doing something else, like cricket. Or in the gym or the shower . . . .

Madame's voice surged in on me.

'So, to recap, the past participle of *acquérir* is . . . ? Sophie?'

Oh, doom . . . .

'So, what are you going to do next week while I'm tied up with my frog?' I asked Chloe later in the locker-room.

'This and that,' she said dismissively. 'Le Becq's wants some more watercolours – I might do a few of those. Anyway, it'll be nice having a break from you.'

'Likewise, I'm sure!' I grinned, and checked my watch. Only one more careers lecture to go ('How to fill in Job Applications and Impress People') before we could escape.

Just then, someone tapped me on the shoulder.

'You're Sophie Sampson, aren't you?' said a toothy third year.

'So?'

'Miss Shue wants to see you in her office right away,' she said, disappearing back into the flow of kids surging out into the corridor.

I *hate* it when people say that. If you know someone 'wants to see you', you immediately feel guilty because you think you've done something wrong, even if you haven't. Especially if it's Miss Shue.

Miss Shue has a face like a prune and gives the impression that landing the job of careers teacher at Bishop Collard Comprehensive is the most exciting thing that's ever happened to her. And the agony of facing her was worse this time, because I *did* know what I'd done.

'Save me, Chloe!' I muttered, clutching her shoulder and pretending to drown.

'Oh, go face your responsibilities!' she smirked.

So I did.

* * *

'I won't keep you, Sophie,' said Miss Shue, shuffling piles of paper around on her desk, which was a habit of hers. 'I just needed a chat with you about your A-levels.'

Chat? Spanish Inquisition, more like.

'Yes,' I muttered, staring at my shoes. 'I still haven't decided.'

'That's all well and good,' said Miss Shue, exasperated before we'd even begun, 'but you're the only fifth-former who hasn't handed in her options. You *must* think about it. Plan ahead. Decide what career you're heading for, and what exams you need to get there. I mean, what do you want to *do?*'

She was looking really fierce now. 'Am I getting through to you?'

'Yes, Miss Shue,' I mumbled. I knew what was coming next. Jobs Don't Grow on Trees.

'Jobs don't grow on trees, you know,' she went on. 'Your grades could all be as good as Chloe's; you could take practically anything in the sixth form and do well. But you *have* to decide where you're going in life.'

How could I tell her? How do you explain to a teacher that just because you get good marks at something doesn't mean you actually *like* it? The reason I couldn't decide was because I wasn't particularly enthralled by *any* school subjects.

Miss Shue glared at me.

'I'll be honest with you, Sophie. There are those who think you've got great potential, but you're wasting it because you just don't apply yourself. You owe it to yourself to get the best qualifications you can. You could go far. The trouble is, you don't *think*.'

I was dumbstruck. It was true; I knew it. But I didn't see what *I* could do about it. I wanted to stay on – I just didn't want to *study*.

There was only one thing to do: I put on my sincere face. You have to humour them when they get like this. 'I'll give it serious thought, Miss Shue,' I promised.

I *think* she believed me.

* * *

We stopped off at Chloe's on the way back to my house to dump her stuff. I was still replaying the interview with Miss Shue, putting in all the things I hadn't had the nerve to say. I looked at Chloe.

'Of course, it's all right for Miss Teacher's Pet,' I thought mutinously.

'What about economics, French and German? That's a

good combination,' Miss Teacher's Pet suggested. 'It could be your passport to Europe. You could go on to do business studies – we could go to college together.'

'I'll think about it,' I said.

But I didn't. I put it to the back of my mind, hoping that an answer would suddenly pop out at me one day – which is exactly what happened, eventually. However, I now know it's a lousy way to handle decisions. Some don't submit without a struggle.

'What about you?' I asked Chloe. 'You could be an artist, you know.'

She pulled on her oldest sweater and started to brush her hair back into a pony-tail.

'There's no money in it,' she mumbled, her scrunchie hair-elastic wedged between clenched teeth. 'Let's go down and see if there's any fodder.'

At Chloe's, you never knew what you'd be eating. It could just as easily be a takeaway, a lentil soufflé or nothing at all – which was why my mum provided such huge servings when Chloe came to tea.

'Don't you *dare* leave any food when we get to my house,' I warned. 'Mum's really put herself out to pander to your finicky food fads.'

To be fair, my mum's excursions into the vegetarian appendix of her cookery book had been quite successful. At Chloe's, nobody seemed to have the time for *haute cuisine* – beans on toast was the dish consumed with the greatest frequency *there*.

'You do realise she puts Oxo cubes in everything, don't you?' I said, baiting her.

Chloe wasn't fooled. 'No, she doesn't,' she said. 'She checked it out with me ages ago. Your mum's OK, Sophie – did you know that?'

I did. But it does you good to be reminded from time to time.

We found Mrs P in the kitchen, dwarfed beside an economy-size packet of disposable nappies, and copying down the manufacturer's address.

'Hey, Hattie,' grinned Chloe, thumping down her rucksack. 'Is there something you haven't told us?'

I loved it when Clo spoke to her mother like that – mine would never have stood for it.

'Come off it, Coco,' she replied, good-naturedly. 'I only bought them because I'm going to complain about the blurb. Anyway, they won't go to waste – I'll send them down to the Women's Refuge.'

'What blurb?' asked Chloe, plonking herself down beside her.

'Just look at this,' said Mrs P. 'See that? "Environment-friendlier"! Exactly what do they think that means? How many trees do you suppose it takes to make these blasted things?'

She took a drag on her Gauloise before continuing.

'Then there's disposal – they don't rot down properly. You're dumping untreated sewage, *plus* there's pollution from the manufacture. And they have the gall to put "environment-friendlier" on the packaging. I *ask* you!'

She exhaled through her mouth, sending out a narrow shaft of smoke. 'How stupid do they think women are to fall for all this guff?'

'Suppose you use old-fashioned nappies, then? What about all the bleach?' said Chloe, spoiling for a juicy discussion.

'True,' said Harriet. 'I used those with you, and a damned nuisance they were, too – excuse my French. I suppose reproduction of the human race is bad news for the planet, however you look at it.'

'Definitely,' agreed Chloe. Then she changed tack suddenly. 'You're *supposed* to have given up the dreaded weed. Again.'

'I have,' said Mrs P, stubbing out her cigarette, even though I didn't think she'd finished it. 'It was only the one. To calm my indignation.'

'Don't you know what you're doing to yourself?' said Clo, with barely-concealed anger. 'How you can claim to be green *and* smoke is beyond me.'

'Lay off, Coco! It's not the same thing at all,' said her mum.

They stared intently at each other for a moment.

'Just stop it, Mum. OK?' Chloe was deadly serious.

'OK,' echoed Mrs Prentice meekly, as if Chloe were the mother and she were the child.

'She hates it when I call her "Mum",' Chloe confessed later on the way across to my house. 'It makes her feel guilty. I can talk her into anything if I call her Mum.'

'Blackmailer!'

'Well, you've got to, sometimes,' Clo said, all big eyes and candour. 'She's her own worst enemy!'

'There are times when I find you unbearably smug, Chloe Prentice,' I thought as we walked along. 'You're so sure of yourself. So much in control of your life.'

I didn't know then quite how fragile Chloe's grasp on her destiny was to prove.

4

The night the sky fell in

I can remember really clearly walking down Woodman Avenue; we weren't speaking much. I was wrapped in thoughts of my own, lulled by the soft evening sounds – the faint purr of traffic on the bypass and the occasional whirr of a lawnmower.

I was nervous about Hugh, yes; but I didn't have a premonition of disaster or anything. I can't claim *that*. I've thought and thought about it, but there was no hint, no feeling of impending doom. Everything was just *ordinary* before we got to the disco.

Life's funny like that – you think you know someone, and then they go and do something so out of character, so unpredictable that it leaves you gasping.

We'd got ready at Clo's. It was one of her mother's evenings on duty at the Women's Refuge, so it was peaceful enough after she'd zoomed out to save the world. We hadn't avoided a lecture altogether, though.

'Let me know if they're using those little plastic cups, Coco,' she'd said. 'If they do, I'll get Josie to bring it up at the PTA. I know they're cheap, but you can't instil a sense of responsibility in kids these days if you're squeezing the life out of the environment yourself.'

'Sure thing, Hattie,' said Clo.

'I'm *serious*,' said Mrs P. 'Do you realise, Sophie, some of these plastics *never* break down? Can you imagine it? We'll be up to our knees in polystyrene beakers by the Day of Judgment! Schools need to set a good example. Am I right – or am I right?'

'I *am* on your side, you know,' Chloe assured her, hoping vainly to head off a more lengthy discourse.

'People can't cope with real life these days. *Oh*, no. They want convenience and disposability. They don't want to kill a pig themselves – they want someone else to do it, and shrink-wrap it so it doesn't even look like an animal anymore. And they won't take responsibility for what they've done. They'll destroy the planet for the sake of not getting their ickle-pretty hands messy.'

Chloe grimaced behind her mum's back and rolled her eyes heavenwards.

'Hey, did I show you my letter in the *Guardian?* They printed it!' said Mrs P, grabbing her bag in one hand and, with the other, attempting to leaf through a floppy and unco-operative newspaper.

'Oh blast – that's yesterday's. Look, I'll show you when I get home. I'll be late if I don't get going.'

She made for the back door. 'Have a nice time,' she said, disappearing. 'Don't forget about the cups.'

The air was dusty and mild and smelt of tarmac; we could have done with some rain. I glanced at Chloe, who looked very cool, very assured. All I could think of was whether my hair needed brushing, and should I have worn the green? Still, I'd done my best.

'You look really pretty,' Clo said. 'You honestly do. Stop

worrying.'

I smoothed down my skirt, wondering what Hugh's verdict would be. 'This is as good as it gets, buster,' I decided.

We heard the far-off throb of the music long before we got to the school – no doubt the local residents would be complaining again. The disco had been going about an hour, and we felt we'd pitched our arrival about right. You *have* to time these things.

We crossed the carpark, past the headteacher's Volvo, a few battered Escorts belonging to the teachers, a handful of cars borrowed for the evening from parents who were probably bitterly regretting it at this moment, and, nearest the hall, Bruno's scarlet MGB Roadster. Chrome-finished.

Andrew Finch, Gregor Lumb and a six-pack of Hofmeister vanished around the side of the bike-sheds as we approached. We ignored them.

Inside, the music was deafening – the hall was pretty full, and somebody had been making a pointless effort to decorate it. The room smelt vaguely of cigarette smoke, despite the vigilance of the prowling Wiggie.

Miss Brown (CDT) was manning the soft drinks, and there was the usual smattering of younger teachers bopping embarrassingly in their I'm-eighteen-really – I-only-look-thirty-six routine. Of Hugh, no sign.

'There they are!' cried Chloe, steering me by the elbow on an erratic and bumpy course across to the far side, where Tamsin, Cass, Rosie and Emily were standing around trying to look casual. And failing.

We spent the next half-hour jigging about unenthusiastically in a little group, trying to lip-read and wondering when someone would ask us for a dance. There was some interesting viewing, though. It was the first time we'd been to a disco with the sixth-formers, and some of them you'd never have recognised out of school uniform.

Cass, too, looked quite . . . surprising.

'Does your mum know what you're wearing?' I bellowed in her ear.

'Oh, about half-past ten,' she shouted back.

Chloe elbowed me and pointed out Ben Vine in the corner. He'd come in the most amazing assortment of clothes – checked trousers, checked shirt, checked tie and checked sports jacket – none of which matched.

'I bet he thinks he looks really cool!' I sniggered, congratulating myself on a lucky escape. And then I saw out of the corner of my eye Chloe stiffen. She pulled at my sleeve, and we zigzagged across to the side-door, which stood open behind its heavy blue curtains. We slipped outside into the quadrangle.

It was blissfully cool out there; it felt just as if some giant had turned down the volume and turned up the lights all at once. I blinked at Clo questioningly.

'I saw Hugh come out here,' she explained, peering around, confused.

I ssshhhed her frantically – I was sure she was talking too loudly. You always do when you come out of a disco.

There were quite a few kids outside getting fresh air. Jane Soper and some other girls we didn't particularly know were having a discreet smoke behind the boys' toilet block, and there were a few amorous couples welded together against the wall. But Hugh wasn't anywhere to be seen.

'That's odd,' said Clo.

Perhaps she'd been mistaken; perhaps it had been someone else. Maybe he'd gone back in while we were navigating our way across the dance-floor. I leant back against the wall, which was still warm from the sun. You could *feel* the pounding beat of the music in the masonry; my heart was pretty much the same way at the thought of encountering Hugh. Still, there it was. Or rather, there he wasn't.

'I'll be back in a minute,' said Clo. 'I'm going to the loo. Coming?'

I shook my head and stayed where I was, waiting for my heart to slow down, and taking the opportunity to rehearse a few opening lines with which to dazzle the said Mr Carter.

Just then I heard raised voices from somewhere on my right. As if with one accord, everyone in the courtyard paused to listen.

At first, it was just an angry fuzz of sound, but then I recognised who it was. It was Bruno Villebonne and Roo. They had prised themselves apart and were now facing each other squarely, accusingly. Whatever the matter was must have been so bad that they didn't care if anyone saw them.

As if from nowhere, more people began to filter into the quad until the unhappy couple had quite an audience. I felt Chloe arrive at my elbow. She was standing tensely; she hated scenes.

'But I only said . . . .'

'Yes, but what about *me*? What about my feelings? Did you think of that, you . . . you . . . *bastard?*' Roo was almost screeching. 'You're an arrogant *swine!*'

'Calm down!' Bruno shouted, grabbing her by the shoulders.

Roo was hysterical. Her hair was untidy, and she was pinkish around the nostrils like you are when the tears are about to start but you don't want it to happen at any price.

She shook herself free.

'Why *can't* I have some freedom? What makes you think I want to be saddled with *you* at Oxford?' Bruno was yelling.

Roo was quaking visibly, her fists clenching and unclenching. There was a silence, and when she spoke again it was in a horribly calm voice, loaded with venom. And it really carried. Everyone heard what she said. She meant it to.

'Oxford?' she said, with a bitter little laugh. 'Don't give me *that!* You only got in because of the rugby. You're pathetic, Bruno Villebonne – all groin and no brain. And let me tell you – the groin isn't that hot, either.'

And with that, she turned on her heel and walked slowly away.

Bruno adjusted his jacket, scowling, and then strode off in the other direction.

Chloe watched him, letting out a slow whistle between her teeth.

'Roo one – Bruno nil!' I said.

The other kids in the courtyard waited a moment, then dispersed as quietly as they'd come. I felt very sorry for Bruno at that moment, humiliated in front of the school like that; and Roo had only succeeded in making herself look a queen-sized shrew.

Wiggie emerged hurriedly and glared around him, but as the action was all over by then, he just shrugged and went back into the hall. I was about to do the same – sometimes you need to immerse yourself in something to take away a nasty taste in your mouth. Then another incident happened that drove it out of my mind.

My eye swept past a boy and a girl – they were sitting

entwined on a low wall. He had one arm around her and the other sliding casually down over her buttock. I had just registered the fact that the girl was Gillian Pitt, and that she seemed to be offering little or no resistance, when my world ended. For that night, anyway.

The boy was Hugh.

They say that realisation dawns, but this one didn't. It drenched me like a bucket of scalding water followed by a bucket of ice. Everything went into slow motion. I couldn't move, but I couldn't tear my eyes away from them, either.

Hugh smiled and said something to Gillian. Gill laughed and whispered in his ear. Then she eased his hand back up to her waist and they sauntered back into the hall.

The music was still pouring out into the summer sky. They were playing oldies now, smoochy songs. It was a Beatles' number – *Yesterday*. I stayed out there an age, leaning back limply against the sun-warmed brick, listening to the words as if I'd never heard them before, and really *feeling* them.

Hugh. And Gillian Pitt. *Gill*, for goodness' sake? She wasn't even that pretty. I was crushed. It made me feel about six years old. I was near to tears and I wanted to go home.

When I turned to Chloe for moral support, to my surprise she wasn't there. She must have slipped tactfully away when she saw how upset I was. But, then again, wouldn't she have *said* something? It wasn't quite like Clo.

It took some effort to tug together the shreds of my self-confidence and go into the hall, but I had to. My bag and jacket were in there.

You know how it is when you go back into a dim room – your eyes take a while to adjust. Perhaps that was why

I didn't pick up on a certain tension in the atmosphere until I'd blundered almost all the way back to the girls. I was desperate to grab my things, find Chloe and go. Selfish, I'll admit, but all I wanted was a shoulder to cry on; I thought I felt as bad as it was possible to feel.

But I was wrong. I felt a whole lot worse when I found her.

'Where's Clo?' I mouthed at Cassie, who was drinking her Coke (from the can, not a plastic cup) with a distracted look on her face.

'There!' she shouted, jerking her head to the left. 'Didn't you *know?*'

It was only then that I noticed how many people had themselves stopped dancing to watch the couple swaying slowly and passionately in each other's arms in the centre of the floor.

For one agonising moment I thought it was Hugh and Gill. Then I saw it was Bruno.

And Chloe.

5

Of frogs . . .

The next morning, I woke up early. I could tell it was going to be a beautiful day from the way the sun was slanting through the curtains.

I didn't move. There was no breeze coming through the open window, only the distant chink of bottles and the whirr of a milk-float.

Far above, I could hear a plane; its engines made the sort of faint, echoey sound that only happens when the sky is empty of cloud and it's going to be hot.

For a moment, I was a small child again, with the summer stretching endlessly and blissfully ahead. And then, like a lead weight, the memory of last night suddenly crashed down on top of me.

I cringed as I remembered it. Hugh. Chloe. Bruno. What a mess! 'At least Hugh never realised I liked him,' I thought, rolling over to a more comfortable position. I could at least be grateful for that. Nor had I made a public fool of myself, like Roo. But Gill Pitt? What did he see in *her?*

I was bruised, stunned. After all that loving and hoping, you can't just switch off someone in your mind. *But,* I decided, hauling myself up in bed, I'll just have to. Chloe, though, was another matter . . . .

The thought of Clo churned in my stomach, and I wondered why. Then the reason hit me. I was *jealous*. I'd always thought of myself as the prettier of the two of us, the one more likely to get a boyfriend. Yet here she was beating me to it! It stung. It *really* stung. After all the effort I'd put into winning Hugh, she – the one supposedly not interested in boys – was the one to scoop the school prize.

And Bruno . . . B*runo*, for heaven's sake! Of all the boys at Bishop Collard, he was the *last* one I'd have said she'd go for. If I imagined her with anyone at all, it would have been someone intellectual. Clever. Arty. Like Hugh, in fact . . . .

I groaned. This was getting me nowhere. I needed to take my mind off it all. It was just as well that the French students were arriving after lunch today. I'd been dreading it, but perhaps the change would do me good. One thing was certain: I couldn't face Chloe. It was stupid, I know, but I felt betrayed – betrayed and angry. Just then, I didn't think I could say a polite word to her.

I heaved myself out of bed and reread Madame Launay's handout, which was lying on my dressing-table. The student I'd been allocated was called Claude Dubois.

'Well,' I thought, pulling on my new jeans, 'it could be worse.'

'Claude' sounded pretty old-fashioned, but then again he could be good-looking. Perhaps he'd ask me out. And I was off again, imagining . . . .

I'd arranged to leave Bates' early that morning to get to the coach station in time. So I didn't see Chloe at lunch-break when we usually changed shifts, which was a relief, because I was still furious with her.

The coach was late. We were hot and bored, and there's nothing – but *nothing* – to do in a coach station when you have to wait for an hour and a half. We'd sunk to the level of making paper planes from pamphlets about day-trips to Calais, when the students' coach finally turned the corner and pulled wheezily into the bay.

Madame Launay greeted her opposite numbers with great enthusiasm and a kiss on each cheek. We were so wound up by this time that we found it hysterically funny; we sniggered like idiots.

'We're not supposed to give our students French kisses, are we?' whispered Cassie in horror.

'*That's* not a French kiss, you dope!' said Tamsin, digging her in the ribs as our French exchange partners poured out of the coach, looking even hotter, more tired and fed-up than we were. And, it has to be said, older and more sophisticated and altogether rather intimidating, really.

'Which one's Claude?' I wondered.

They were grabbing their rucksacks and retrieving their luggage while Madame Launay and the other teachers checked off names on a list. Then she called for order, and, after explaining the week's programme in both languages, started to pair us off.

Brian got the dishy boy in cords. Cass got a short girl with sunglasses and a worried expression. Julie got a tall, model-like brunette with a bust of Alpine proportions.

And I was going to get Claude. Which one was mine? Where *was* he? As Madame Launay read out his name, I stared frantically, waiting to see which hand would move to pick up which suitcase and head my way.

And when it did, the fact didn't register. Cass says I did a classic double-take.

'*Bonjour*,' said an attractive blonde-haired girl, proffering her hand. '*Je m'appelle Claude* . . . .'

Monsieur Dubois was, as they say, the feminine article.

* * *

From that point on, the week disappeared in a blur of organised activities, most of which we Brits were roped into.

Claude and I got on well; her English was depressingly good. Had I sounded as fluent in my GCSE oral, as I booked into a hotel room and exchanged a jumper two sizes too big? Probably not.

Claude chain-smoked and seemed desperate for holiday romance. She took far more interest in the boys in our form than we did, and they were certainly flattered by her attentions. They *had* improved enormously during the past year, it was true – if she could see something we couldn't, perhaps they deserved a second glance.

I was surprised to find myself actually *enjoying* Claude's stay, even though it meant having Kate share my bedroom. One of the best trips was an outing to the ladies' quarter-finals at Wimbledon, where we witnessed what turned out to be one of the most historic and riveting matches of Tennis Fortnight. Madame obviously has connections where it counts.

But even so, I was glad when Thursday came and, with it, a free afternoon.

I met up with Cass, Julie and Tamsin at McDonald's. Only Tamsin had an exchange partner she couldn't get along with. Her family had taken Françoise pick-your-own strawberrying – a favourite treat in Tami's family – but she had been 'insulted and demeaned' at 'being forced to do farm work'.

'I think she's homesick, really,' Tamsin said (rather generously, I thought). She poked her straw through the slit in the plastic lid of her Coke. 'But I don't know which of us'll be gladder when she goes.'

'By the way, Bruno and Roo are coming to the party tomorrow evening,' said Cass. 'Madame Launay invited him because he's half-French.'

I pricked up my ears at this.

'Roo?' I said. 'I thought they'd split up.'

Cass's face fell. 'Sorry, Sophe – I was sure you'd know,' she said, going pink. 'Clo was a one-night stand. He's back with Roo now – for keeps, Roo says. She's wearing a ring. But *he* told Toby they *weren't* engaged. Now, what do you make of *that?*'

Not a lot, as it happened. I hardly listened to the rest of the chatter – my mind was whirling. Suddenly all my irritation towards Chloe vanished. What had Bruno done? How was Clo feeling? I wanted to see her as soon as possible.

'. . . don't you think, Sophe?'

'Yeah, right,' I muttered, vaguely.

Why hadn't she been in touch? Had I offended her or something? Come in, Chloe; this is Sophie calling . . . .

* * *

Claude didn't appear at teatime. Kate explained why when I asked where she was.

'Oh, she's gone to London with some friends – she said her boyfriend had tickets for *Top of the Pops.*'

Boyfriend?

'She'll be back this evening. She said it would be early.'

'So, who's the lucky guy?' I pondered silently, chewing my way through shepherd's pie, traditional British food being the only thing on the Sampson menu this week – for Claude's benefit. 'Robert Tibbs? Alistair Davis? Robin Jones? And why haven't the boys invited any of *us?*'

Last time someone got tickets for *Top of the Pops*, practically the whole class went – in a sisterly, brotherly sort of way, you understand. Even Chloe went.

Yes, *Chloe* . . . whom I could now go and see, since my evening was unexpectedly clear. I finished my meal in undue haste, and made for the door.

'I'm just off to Clo's, Mum,' I shouted, pulling on my denim blouson.

'Hang on a moment,' she called out from the kitchen.

I went back to investigate.

'I forgot to mention,' Mum said, glancing up from the chopping-board. 'Chloe won't be at home – she's sitting for Ruth and Tony.'

But that was *our* job – something we always did together. I must have looked peeved because Mum rushed on to explain.

'They wanted a sitter at short notice; I thought you'd be tied up with Claude, so I told Tony to try Chloe. He was really lucky – he managed to get a cancellation at Clancy's.'

Mum took a long sip of tea from her mug. 'Ruth needed a break – they've had another of those cranky letters.'

Oh, no. Poor Ruth. I thought the flak had stopped long ago.

'How is she?' I asked.

Mum was picking the sludgy meat off the carcass of

yesterday's chicken and feeding it to Puddy Tat, who was on tiptoes beside her, clawing his way up the cupboard door.

'Oh, she's laughing it off – you know Ruth. But it's badly upset her.'

Mum gave a sudden angry snort and thumped her fist down on the chopping-board, sending Puddy scooting into the hall with a fat tail.

'It makes me livid!' she said.

You could tell she'd been brooding over it all afternoon.

'How can people be so heartless? Ruth's waited twenty years for those kids! I don't know how many operations she's had, how many treatments she's been on. Heaven knows, she's suffered enough. It's sickening!'

It really was.

'Did you see the letter?' I asked.

'Yes – she brought it over this afternoon. She made light of it. But really, Sophie! "Taking children from their national culture and heritage" indeed! Where's the heritage in wallowing in your own urine, two to a cot?'

'Some people are just sick,' I said. 'They don't think.'

'No,' said Mum. 'They don't.'

If Ruth's anonymous correspondent had been in our kitchen at that moment, I reckon he'd have been in much the same condition as Mum's chicken by now. Puddy slunk warily back in.

'I'm sorry,' she added, wiping her hands on a dish-cloth, 'I should have asked you first – I shouldn't have assumed you'd be busy with Claude.'

'That's OK, Mum,' I said. 'I didn't know I was going to have an empty evening.'

And, as it turned out, that most definitely *wasn't* what I got.

6

. . . and princes

'Hi, Clo!' I said brightly when she answered the door.

You see, I'd worked out my strategy. Which was to proceed as if nothing had happened – no need for her to know that this time yesterday I was hating her guts. I'd just sound her out. See how she was. And how she was, was strained.

'No Claude?' she asked.

'No Claude,' I said, and went in.

The twins, Edward and Sarah, had taken advantage of Chloe's absence to get out the cornflakes, which were now in a pile on the lounge carpet. Sarah was trying valiantly to scoop them back into the plastic liner, with a visible lack of success.

'Oops!' she said, grinning up at us sheepishly.

* * *

One hour, four glasses of milk and six Postman Pat stories later, peace descended and we could finally talk.

'So,' I said bravely, breaking an awkward silence – an unusual thing for us – 'how are things?'

'Not so good,' Clo said simply, staring at her trainers.

'Do you want to talk about it?' I asked carefully.

She didn't answer for a minute. She looked so unlike herself that I was starting to worry.

'Yes,' she said at length, 'I'd appreciate that.' And then, to my horror, a tear plopped on to her knee.

I didn't know what to do. I'm useless if anyone gets emotional; I can't handle stuff like that. What made it worse was that *I* felt guilty, as if it was my anger that had hurt her.

She blew her nose. 'I'll make a coffee first,' she said, and headed for the kitchen.

I put on a CD – it kind of filled the gaps. And while I waited for her, I stared at Ruth and Tony's collection of family photographs, frantically wondering all the while what on earth to say next.

The photos were mounted in ribboned frames, and they always made me feel weepy. The oldest was of Ruth and Tony on their wedding day. Honestly, the trousers! The shoes! They looked so incredibly young.

There was a long lapse of time before the next shot – a fuzzy print of them holding Edward and Sarah (then Sergiu and Mihaela) in the orphanage near Bucharest, and beside it, a picture of them together when they appeared on *Panorama*.

Last of all, there was a beautiful professional portrait. The children were very little, but they looked so happy. Edward had the goofiest grin – you couldn't help but smile when you saw it. But even *that* didn't work its magic on me tonight.

Chloe returned with the coffee, and we sat down facing

each other. Then we talked. And talked.

I don't know how I could have been so *blind*. After all, looking back, the signs were there – I just hadn't picked them up. Chloe, it now transpired, had been nursing a secret passion for Bruno Villebonne since we were in the first form. She'd never said anything because she knew what we all thought of him. She knew we'd laugh at her.

After the Big Row at the disco, Chloe had followed Bruno back into the hall, almost without thinking. He'd suddenly turned and, seeing her, asked her to dance. She'd always assumed that he didn't know she existed, so for her it was a dream come true. And although she would have wished for the circumstances to be different, how could she refuse?

They'd danced a few smoochy numbers together (which was where I'd come in and stomped out). And once he was certain that *everyone* had seen him with the girl who had the reputation of being the most intellectual in the school, he'd swept her away in his red MGB Roadster (chrome-finished) to the Weary Fox at Lye's Green.

For the whole evening, Chloe kept wondering whether or not this was the start of something; Bruno was charming but detached – as if his thoughts were elsewhere. Which, in all honesty, they probably were.

And then, on Saturday evening, Roo (whom Chloe only knew by sight) rang her up in a high temper to tell her that she and Bruno were together again and Clo had better keep her hands off him. A *long* way off. How Roo had got him back after all she'd said to him was one of the unsolved mysteries of the universe.

'You're always telling me you can't love someone you don't really know,' I said. 'You only knew Bruno from the outside.'

I thought it might help if I recycled some of Chloe's past advice to me; you know, be green and all that. It probably didn't help – she never said a thing.

'I can't believe you liked him,' I said, trying again. 'I mean, you're so brainy and he's so . . . so *physical*.'

'Well, thanks a lot!' she retorted, sniffing. 'Look who's talking! Who's got Mel Gibson posters all over her bedroom?'

I had the grace to blush. Still, there was one thing we agreed on. 'Bruno's a louse,' I said.

Ruth had left us a plate of buns, the sort I usually find boring. But tonight I kept eating and eating and eating.

Chloe began to cry.

'I'm starting to think so, too,' she said.

'A*nd* Roo,' I said with my mouth full, spraying crumbs all over the cushions.

* * *

So it was a pretty depressing evening, all told. Chloe felt bad and I did, too. We felt so very bad that it was actually a welcome intrusion when we heard a squeaky little voice carolling out, 'Chlo-eeee! Soph-ieeee! Edward's wet the bed – *again!*'

Well, it gave us something to do.

We put a brave face on it when Ruth and Tony came bouncing in, all smiles, at eleven.

'How have they been?' Ruth asked as Tony got ready to see us home.

'Great!' I said. 'Apart from the washing in the bath, that is. They're sleeping like angels.'

And a good night's sleep was exactly what Chloe and

I needed to soothe our frayed nerves and help us forget that men existed. In the morning, we'd feel better.

But I was wrong about that, too. I mean, how could I have known that things were going to get worse? *Much* worse.

7

Results

It's very hard to cope with someone who refuses to cheer up.

Chloe was becoming – to put it bluntly – a king-sized pain. I hadn't expected her to react like this; she was normally so mature about things. I'd put the Hugh episode behind me, and I suppose I expected Clo to forget Bruno just as quickly. But *she* wasn't *me*. She always took things so seriously, and, besides, her adoration of the Big B went back *years*.

It was hard going – for both of us – and I simply couldn't chivvy her out of it.

'Cheer up, Clo!' I'd joke. 'Don't vent your PMT on me!'

But it didn't work – in fact, she really went for me when I said that.

If you were to ask me what I did that summer holiday, I don't think I could really tell you. I lazed around, worked extra hours in Bates' and went with Cass, Julie and Tamsin on a week's Improve-Your-Tennis course at the leisure centre.

The main attraction of the latter was the decidedly

fanciable coach, Oliver.

'The accuracy of your forehand is really improving, Sophie,' he'd say, encouragingly.

'See? It's *you* he likes,' Cass would whisper, dead jealous.

'No, he doesn't,' I'd protest, despairingly. 'He's just nice to everyone.' Which, indeed, he was.

Oliver had great legs and a great smile. He smiled a lot. So I did, too.

Result: Zilch. Was this guy vaccinated against charm or something?

'He's just the total *professional*,' said Cass, breathily.

All the smiling in the world didn't manage to change Love One into Love All by the end of the week. So we hung up our racquets with a sigh and went home.

And somewhere in the middle of the vacation, I went to Dyfed on a family holiday. I swore it was going to be my last. I mean, I didn't *ask* to be related to JG. I put up with him all year – don't you think it's stretching the bonds of sisterly loyalty just a little to expect me to devote a solid *week* to him?

Anyway, Dyfed in the rain is marginally more enjoyable than having your leg amputated. Especially when you can't escape from JG's constant whingeing about the joke book he's forgotten, or from Kate, who's developed a tummy bug which she generously shares with her loved ones.

Or from Dad, who is only used to JG in small doses and can't understand why what was supposed to be a relaxing week has turned out more stressful than being at the office. Mum, of course, just smiles while secretly tearing her hair out.

I fervently hoped Chloe would have got it out of her system by the time I came home, but I hoped in vain. I was starting to get anxious about her as well as irritated;

even Mum had noticed that she wasn't herself.

'She's worried about the GCSE results,' I lied. 'She's got her heart set on graphic design.'

'Poor dear,' said Mum.

I was less compassionate.

'Snap out of it, you moron!' I said. '*No* guy's worth this much grief.'

'Too right!' Chloe muttered. 'Men are just *swine*. I never want to see another one again.'

I looked at her and sighed inwardly. 'This is what comes of having a nutty mother,' I thought. With motivation like this, you can appreciate why I started spending more time with Cassie.

In fact, it was while I was playing tennis with Cass that I decided what subjects to take in the sixth. We were just knocking the ball back and forth and I was idly thinking about life, the universe and everything, when it suddenly struck me. My decision, I mean; not the ball. I'd shoved it to the back of my mind, but it must have been fermenting away in there – and suddenly, out popped the answer.

Primary teaching. That's what I *really* wanted to do.

I had an overwhelming feeling of relief; and having settled on that, the right A-levels just fell into place.

'Miss Shue'll be delighted with me,' I thought gleefully, returning Cass's shot with an unintentional forehand lob which had so much extra energy put into it that the ball landed in a tree.

'*Sophie!*' Cass shouted crossly.

We never did get the ball down.

*   *   *

I thought the twenty-third of August would never come, but it did. Too soon.

I'd arranged to meet Chloe to collect the results – they were posted to us, but if you went to the school office in person, you could find out that much earlier. Clo had said she'd call around at half-past nine, but she didn't. By a quarter to ten, my nerves were shot to pieces.

'Ring her,' said Mum. 'Perhaps she's forgotten.'

'Forgotten the *results?* No way,' I said firmly, dialling her number.

The phone brrr-brrred into emptiness; no reply. I couldn't stand the suspense any longer.

'I'll just go,' I said. 'She's probably waiting at the school. If she *does* turn up, tell her I've gone, will you?'

'Would you like me to run you down?' asked Mum.

'No thanks.'

She must be joking. This was something I had to do on my *own*.

I was trembling like a leaf by the time I got to the school. There were a few fifth-formers and teachers hanging around the office and carpark, but nobody I really knew, and I was glad about that. I took a deep breath, pushed open the office door and went in.

Mrs Barber, the secretary, threw me a warm smile and flicked through a sheaf of envelopes.

'Here you are, dear!' she beamed. 'I think you'll be pleased.'

I went outside and found a secluded corner. My hands were sticky and wouldn't work properly. My heart was thumping. I wanted to know, but at the same time I *didn't*, either.

After about a hundred years, I managed to pull out the little computerised slip and read the results. Pass – pass

– pass – pass – pass – pass – and maths? Yes! A pass! A definite pass! Fail? In what? Oh, chemistry . . . well, I'd expected that. Who cares about chemistry, anyway?

The relief drenched me like a tidal wave, and I couldn't help grinning as I sat there, waiting for my blood pressure to normalise.

'Wotcha get, Sophe?' asked Jane Soper, coming out of the office.

'It was OK,' I said, smiling like a baboon. 'I just want to tell Mum first.'

'Suit yourself,' said Jane, stalking down the drive. Then a thought struck me, and I rushed back into the office.

'Has Chloe been in yet? Chloe Prentice?'

Mrs Barber checked her list.

'No, dear, she hasn't. But she has to come in person – I can't let you take her slip for her. Rules, you know.'

'No, no – I understand. That's OK,' I said hurriedly.

* * *

'Don't make so much fuss!' I wished silently, as my family whooped excitedly around me. JG whipped the results slip out of Mum's hand and danced about with it.

'Careful!' I shrieked. 'You can't get a duplicate.'

Mum rang Dad at work – but how he could hear her with all the noise going on I'll never know. He was delighted. I, on the other hand, felt ashamed; I hadn't realised until then how proud my parents were of me.

'We'll go out for a meal to celebrate,' he promised when I took the phone. 'Well done, Sprog!'

I must have been happy, because I didn't even mind when he called me that.

'Bye, Dad. See you later,' I said, putting the receiver down. It rang immediately under my hand, and I picked it up.

'Sophie?' said Chloe's voice.

'Hold on.' I put my palm over the mouthpiece, and bellowed 'Shut up!' into the room. Instant calm.

'Sorry about that,' I said, returning to the telephone. 'It's these children. They're just so . . . *childish* sometimes.'

'Sophie, I need to see you. N*ow.* Can you come round? Mum's out. Five minutes, OK?'

She sounded really odd. The grin was still stuck on my face, but the flippancy just kind of drained out of it.

'Mum, that was Clo,' I said. 'I'm going round to her place. We'll eat there, OK?'

Somehow I just *knew* we weren't going to be back for lunch. It was the wrong thing to say to my mum, but what could I do?

'Sophie Anne, you two were supposed to be eating *here.* You treat this place like a restaurant. I'd appreciate a little consideration sometimes. Just *what* am I supposed to do with the kidney-bean casserole?'

A guilt trip was all I needed.

'Sorry, Mum. You can stick it in the freezer, can't you?' I gave her a quick peck on the cheek. 'I'll be back later. Look after my results.'

The slip had by now been transformed into a paper plane and was winging its way around the hall. Mum marched into the fray to retrieve it, and I was out of there.

Call it woman's intuition if you like, but as I walked over to Chloe's, instead of feeling happy I was full of dread. Absolute gloom. Impenetrable. I couldn't explain it.

I rang the bell. 'I'm sure everything's OK,' I tried to convince myself while I waited in the porch, a gibbering idiot. Was it heck.

* * *

'You're *what?*'

I didn't want to believe what I'd heard. Perhaps it wasn't a sensitive way to react, but I couldn't help it. Chloe just sat there, looking very, very tired. Tired and old. But her eyes were bright.

I wanted to laugh. It was a joke, right? A bad dream? *Candid Camera?* April Fool's Day? Then I looked at her, and I knew it wasn't.

It took time for the news to register. When it did, it hit me with the force of an Intercity 125. I felt shocked and angry and bitterly jealous, all mixed up together. I sat there and kept my mouth shut, totally lost for words. What did she hope I was going to do? Wave some magic wand? How dare she ruin my day of triumph, anyway?

I eventually managed to get a grip on my emotions. 'Sophie Sampson – you're behaving like a little kid,' I lectured myself. 'Calm down. Chloe needs you, and you're no good to anybody in this state. Try your deep-breathing exercises – in, out, in, out. That's better.'

I measured my words carefully before I spoke; although I cleared my throat first, I still sounded husky and odd.

'When did you . . . find out?'

'I've been afraid of it all along. I went to the doctor, and the results came this morning. I just got back.'

So that's where she'd been.

'You forgot the GCSEs,' I said.

'Yeah,' she said flatly. 'I did.'

'How did it happen?' I ventured lamely.

'How do you *think*, you idiot?'

'It was . . . Bruno?'

'Of course it was B*runo!*' she flashed at me, fiercely. 'What do you take me for?'

'You've been sleeping with B*runo?*'

'O*nce*. It was only once.'

'But . . . but you *can't* get pregnant the first time,' I burst out. My words hung on the air, sounding more and more ridiculous with every passing second. Oh, help . . . .

'Does he know?' I pursued.

'Oh, leave it out!'

I was way, *way* out of my depth. What do I say? What do I do? Beam me up, Scottie. Someone. A*nyone*.

I took refuge in attack. 'You didn't tell me you'd slept with him. Why didn't you tell me? W*hy* did you do it?'

For goodness' sake, this was kind of *fundamental*. How could a best friend forget to tell you she's just lost her virginity?

'If you must know,' said Chloe, shooting me a piercing glance, 'I've never regretted anything more in my entire life. I thought if I pretended it hadn't happened, I might feel better. It might go away. That's what *you* do, isn't it? Bury your head in the sand?'

'Go away? Clo, you're out of your tiny mind! This isn't going to just *go away* by its own sweet self. What the heck came over you?'

And gradually, painfully, the whole story unfolded. This was how it had *really* happened.

Bruno had actually been a far cry from the dashing, debonair romeo of Chloe's imagination. He was poor company when he took her to the Weary Fox after the disco; he was angry, and talked about Roo incessantly. He was also more than slightly drunk. In short, a louse. A *drunken* louse.

Part of Chloe was uneasy about having come with a boy she didn't really know to a place she couldn't get home from by herself, but the rest of her clung on to her fantasy superhero. When he stopped on the way home in a dark lay-by and started to fondle her with obvious intentions, she didn't resist.

'Date-rape!' I breathed.

'No,' she said drily. 'You can't pin *that* on him. It's all about facing responsibilities, right? I *let* him do it. I let him.'

'But . . . you . . . .'

'I know, I know,' she said. She looked haggard. 'I was all high principles and stern resolve and all that, but when he started getting heavy, I couldn't handle it. He didn't think about me at all – he just *expected* sex. I suppose I felt I had to live up to his expectations. Be grown-up. I mean, how was I going to get *home?*'

I couldn't believe I was hearing this; I threw out a string of swear words. Well, it made me feel better.

'I'm so *disappointed* in myself, Sophie,' she said miserably. 'I just want to die.'

She looked like she really meant it.

'I wanted to wait until I was married. Honestly, I really did,' she continued. 'But it was like . . . like when you're dead tired and fighting against sleep. Do you know what I mean? You struggle and struggle, and then suddenly it's easier to just give in and go with it.

'He got me really worked up – and then it kind of took over and there was no holding him. I didn't want him to stop. Only I *did*. I suppose, if I'd really wanted, I could have told him to back off. Perhaps I could have kneed him in the groin, or something. But then, he was so strong . . . .'

She groaned. 'Oh, I can't explain it,' she added, very wet

around the eyes, pushing back her hair.

'How was it for you?' I asked. What a *pathetic* question!

'Abysmal, if it's any business of yours,' she said, scrutinising the pattern on her Indian print skirt. 'It was sordid. Horrible. It *hurt*. It made me bleed. He was really angry, really rough, and it was like I was Roo and he was getting his own back on her. Sophie, it was *dreadful*. I never want to see him again. Oh, God,' she finished, simply, and buried her face in her hands. It sounded like a plea.

What do you say at a time like this? How should you react? What do you do? Find out all the gory details, that's what.

'Did he use a condom?' I asked, dreading what I knew I was going to hear.

'No,' said Clo drily.

'You *idiot!*' I almost shouted. 'You could have caught anything. STD. AIDS, even!'

There was an awful silence.

'You don't think so . . . ?'

'I do!'

'It hadn't crossed my mind.'

'Well, it'd better!'

'Bruno couldn't have AIDS.'

'How do *you* know? You don't know how many girls he's slept with. He's been *around*, for goodness' sake.'

'Since when are you Dr Sex Expert?' she snapped. 'What did you expect me to do? Say, "Excuse me, but before we have it off I'd like a list of your past conquests?" '

She looked really bitter. 'Oh, give me a break!'

'What I expected, Chloe,' I said as evenly as my seething temper would allow, 'was that Chloe – who was going to wait until she got married – this sensible Chloe-person would actually do what she damn well told me.'

'Oh, shut up!' she said, tears welling in her eyes.

'Clo,' I went on relentlessly – I couldn't stop. 'What about contraceptives? You're brainy. You're supposed to *know* all that stuff! Don't you read *anything?* You were a Girl Guide. What about "Be Prepared" and all that?'

'Look, I wasn't *expecting* to go the whole way. OK?' said Clo, blubbing. 'I don't carry condoms around, and I wasn't on the Pill, because – can't you understand this? – I wanted to *wait!*'

She spluttered into her hanky.

'Well, why *didn't* you?' I yelled.

There was an excruciating silence, apart from the squelchy, snorty noises someone makes when they're crying *properly*.

I was immediately sorry for laying into her like that. It's just that when something cataclysmic happens, sometimes you're so busy coping with how bad *you* feel that you don't think at all about the other person.

I said sorry; I hadn't meant it that way. There was another awkward silence.

'You don't think I *wanted* it to happen like that?' she sniffed at last.

'I don't know *what* I think,' I admitted, turning aside and staring sightlessly at Chloe's bedroom. As if all that normality could somehow wash away what was happening. As if Chloe's teddy-bear could make everything come right.

Hers was a calm kind of bedroom, with restful colours and soothing posters. But right now its tranquillity seemed to mock us. Over the bed were a couple of Monet prints she'd bought at some art gallery in London on a school trip, and, between them, a few tiny watercolours of garden flowers which she'd been working on recently.

These were the also-rans, the not-quite-good-enoughs; I found them exquisite. Barney had framed the best for sale at Le Becq's, and I'd heard they were going well. ('Boosts the college fund,' Chloe used to say, carelessly.) It hurt to look at them today. To think that all that talent could be wasted – that her dreams of graphic design might never come to be. Stupid, stupid, *stupid* girl.

'I feel like I've let myself down, and I can't ever undo it. I feel . . . *degraded*, Sophie. I've gone against everything I ever hoped for. For what?'

Well, I knew the answer to that one.

For the sky to fall in. Quietly.

8

Dr Sex Expert advises

'How about some lunch?'

'I'm not hungry.'

'Nor me – but I think we *should*. I mean, you're eating for two now . . . unless you'd puke all over the place, of course.'

'I won't. I don't feel sick. You don't always – that's a myth.'

Chloe hoisted herself wearily off the bed, and we traipsed down to the kitchen. I sat her down on the bench, unzipped her a Coke and plunged into the depths of the Prentice larder.

'Beans on toast OK?' I asked, scanning the shelves. No beans. 'Cheese on toast?' I ventured, and turned to the fridge.

I eventually unearthed a slab of no-animal-rennet vegetarian Cheddar behind a tub of mouldy tofu (What's that?) and a plastic bag of rather elderly and whiffy sprouting beans. I then attempted to knock together something to eat.

Whenever I'm worried, I find it helps to go off and do

something completely different, like playing tennis or watching a video – it clears the brain. That was probably why I had the urge to do something – anything – now. 'Worried' being an understatement.

'What's Clo done to me?' I asked myself, my thoughts whizzing giddily around as I poked the granary bread under the grill.

I felt as if the world had exploded under my feet. In many ways, Chloe had been my role model – someone whose opinion I respected, someone I could count on. No matter who came and went, I'd thought Chloe would always be there, knowing what she wanted, knowing where she was going and Being Wise.

While I was pondering all this I was trying to slice up the cheese with an old-fashioned potato peeler, but it was crumbling away. Like my life, really. I felt cast adrift. Bereft. In deep shock. 'If Miss Wisdom's blown it,' I reasoned, 'how can someone ordinary like me have a hope of surviving life unscathed?'

I attacked the cheese with a fruit-knife. Then I lunged at the grill to turn over the bread, just as it set the smoke-detector off – which I then had to fan desperately with a copy of *Women's Rights – Now!* until peace was restored.

Well, you know how it is when you're in someone else's kitchen – you can't find *anything*. (Actually, I can't find anything in my own kitchen, either – I'm not in there that often.)

And the other thing that was tearing me up was that she'd Done It. She was a *woman*, a completed person. And she hadn't told me. Oh, I know she'd said it was no earth-shattering experience, but that wasn't the point. It *still* counted as a notch on her bedpost. I was jealous. Utterly.

As I crouched down to watch the cheese bubbling under

the grill, I grew desperately angry. With life, with me for feeling this way, with Bruno – and, most of all, with Chloe.

I dished the meal up. Pushing an unappealing plateful of toasted cheese at Clo, I ushered her into the lounge, where the chairs were comfier. All without speaking. I wasn't surprised that she wasn't eating it; after one mouthful, I, too, gave up the attempt.

'Chloe . . .' I began awkwardly, but was startled out of my train of thought by Afro-rock music, which suddenly started thudding out from the kitchen we'd just left.

'Coco? Are you in?' called Mrs P's voice.

Chloe pulled herself together quickly.

'In the lounge, Hattie,' she called back.

An elegantly-dressed Harriet stuck her head around the door.

'I thought I'd pop in on my way to Hudson's to see if the results had come second post,' she announced.

'It's not particularly likely, is it?' said Clo.

'Well, I just thought . . .' said her mother, rummaging through her handbag. 'Can't you go down to the school or something?'

'That's what *I* did,' I said, without thinking.

'There you are, then,' said Mrs P brightly. 'Why don't you do that after lunch? It would save us all from getting an ulcer. What did you get, Sophie?' she continued, turning to me.

I told her, catching Clo's What-did-you-go-and-say-that-for? expression out of the corner of my eye.

'That's great. Really great,' said Mrs P. 'Congratulations! By the way,' she added, turning back to Chloe, 'I'm going to the French film at the Multiscreen with Barney tonight. D'you fancy coming? That includes you, too, of course, Sophie.'

Chloe made a face and shook her head.

'No thanks, Hattie. I'm not in a froggy mood.'

'It's Gérard Depardieu.'

'No. No, really . . . .'

'OK. See you later, then. I must fly! Ring me at the office when you've got the results. Don't forget, now.' And Mrs P departed to the strains of Senegalese reggae.

'She's old enough to go without a chaperone. Just this once,' said Chloe, listening as the car engine faded away.

'Heartless beast!' I countered.

For a moment, we'd been bantering just like we used to, before all this happened. But then the real world crowded in on us again. I looked despairingly across at the girl who'd been my best friend for so long, the girl I could insult, laugh with and cry with, the one I'd never really fallen out with. Not seriously, anyway.

'Clo,' I said, 'we've got to *talk*. What are you going to *do?*'

'You do make *exceedingly* bad cheese on toast,' she said. And then, 'If you want the truth, I don't know. I just don't know.'

It was unusual to hear indecision from Chloe Prentice.

'What did the doctor say?'

'He didn't say a lot. He outlined the options, and told me to go away and think about it. I've got to go back and see him this time next week with my decision.'

'Decision?'

'Whether I want to have it or not. But I just don't *know,* Sophie. He said I had to think of my career, my future. I felt pressurised.'

Telling Chloe to do something was a sure-fire way of making her dig her heels in.

'I'm just not *sure*. I've never been pro-abortion, but I've never really thought it through. Yet I just can't see my way out of this. I want to know what *you* think.'

She turned towards me with a hopeful look on her face, as if I could sort everything out.

I put on my best bedside manner. 'You *should* consider it – I mean, he's a doctor. He must know,' I said. 'He wouldn't suggest something that was wrong. Heather O'Connor in the fourth form had an abortion last year – it can't be any big deal.'

I saw her eyes – they were watching me, guardedly.

'Look, Clo,' I went on, 'there's no point getting sentimental about this. It's just a medical procedure. It's not a *baby* yet.' I flinched at saying the word out loud. 'It's just like a sort of tadpole. Having an abortion is only like having your tonsils out. It's an outpatient thingy, isn't it?'

I could see her gaze harden.

'If you had an abortion, no-one'd ever know. Not anyone. Not your mum, not Bruno. Nobody.'

And somehow, at that moment it seemed of vital importance that nobody *should* know. Ever. We had here a convenient carpet under which the whole thing could be swept, with no-one any the wiser. She'd be mad not to take advantage of it.

'I'*d* know,' said Clo.

* * *

I marched her down to the school. She didn't want to go, but we had to do the normal things – keep up appearances.

'I can't. I *can't*! He'll have bragged to his friends. It'll be all over the school by now,' she said in sudden panic, as we reached her gate. I had to pull her through it physically.

'Look – you don't *know* that. I haven't heard any rumours on the grapevine. Anyhow, no-one would believe it of *you*. Perhaps Bruno's a gentleman after all.'

Chloe looked alarmed at the mention of his name aloud in a public place.

'Look, Clo – life goes on. Everyone'll think it's really odd if you don't go in for the results,' I pointed out. 'Come on!'

As we went down Gainsborough Drive I realised that this was the first time Chloe and I had gone anywhere together for *weeks*. I could feel her tension; she looked as if this was her first walk in the outside world since leaving jail.

'So now I know why you've been such a joy to be with recently,' I said.

'So now you know,' she repeated, slinging her bag back over her shoulder. 'Right now, I couldn't care less about the GCSE results.'

Which was a strange attitude to have, I reflected, considering what she'd got. When she opened the envelope, I stared and stared. It was one of those mythical results slips you hear of from time to time – straight A's. I couldn't believe it.

Chloe appeared completely indifferent.

'Look pleased!' I hissed. 'You've got to pretend to look pleased. It's not realistic. Come on – *act!* Eyes and teeth.'

There was a negligible improvement.

There didn't seem any point in going home just yet, so we stopped off at the park. The botanical gardens had plenty of benches, but they all seemed to be taken up by an impressive collection of species of pensioner, all apparently in their dormant phase. We headed instead for the kids' playground.

This was a regular haunt of ours; the offer to take Edward and Sarah there during the holidays was generally good for a few quid. At the time we got there, it was fairly quiet – a few toddlers in the sandpit, and a gang of eight-year-olds trying stunts on their mountain bikes. And pregnant women.

I didn't know what had happened to everyone since yesterday, but suddenly, somehow, every female of childbearing age seemed to be in a state of impending motherhood. From the nearly-due forty-year-old in the scaled-up three-year-old's cutesy dress, to the punk in black leggings and tee-shirt with 'Anarchy' across it in splashy yellow lettering. Chloe couldn't have failed to notice, surely.

We sat on the swings, kicking off idly with our feet. Chloe looked around her gloomily. We were surrounded by so much noise there in the centre of town that we felt strangely private as we swung to and fro, to and fro, to and fro.

Chloe was the first to speak.

'You know,' she said, 'what worried me most wasn't that I could be pregnant. This may seem stupid, but what's *really* got me is that I could throw away my ideals like that. Just give in to some stupid *urge*.'

'Come on, Clo,' I said. 'It's not like it's the first time it's ever happened to anyone.' I listed some GCSE English texts to prove my point – *Far from the Madding Crowd* (Fanny Robin); *Adam Bede* (Hetty Sorrel); *Tess of the D'Urbervilles* (Tess). And a few of our schoolmates, for good measure.

This merely irritated her.

'You don't understand, do you?' she said, swinging. 'You'll never understand how I feel. How could it happen? To *me*? That's what I can't answer. I don't have the answers.

I've never had the answers.'

'But Clo,' I protested, 'that's stupid. You've always been a really definite sort of person. You've always known exactly what you thought. You've *never* been vague.'

I was unprepared for the surprise that flitted across her face when I said that.

'Me? You thought *I* was sure about things?' she asked, a funny sort of half-smile on her lips.

'Well, *yeah!*' I replied defensively.

'Is that how I appear?' she demanded.

'Well, yeah!' I repeated. 'Everyone thinks you're really mature and sensible. I'm sick of teachers saying to me, "Why can't you be more like Chloe?" I've always thought you knew exactly what you believed. I mean, you're great in class debates. People *respect* you.'

This seemed to be news to her. I synchronised our swings, and watched her as we moved in unison through the warm air. She was thinking hard.

'You've got me all wrong, then,' she said, at length. 'I've never *felt* I knew it all. I do think about things, and I've got opinions on stuff. And I know I want to do graphic design at college more than anything else in the world. But that's it, really. I don't know what's right and wrong anymore. I'd like to know. Right now I could do with some absolutes in my life.'

She gazed around the playground. Two toddlers were squabbling in the sandpit, and a young mother was wheeling a sleeping baby from right to left along the path in front of us.

I decided we'd have to move. Chloe's moods were unpredictable today, and now she was getting emotional again.

'I'm not ready for all this,' she said.

It was as I feared; her eyes were filling up again. I pulled her off the swing and we set off into the town centre.

'You're not seriously thinking of having it?' I asked.

'I don't know. I don't see how I can,' she said, pushing her fists deep into her jacket pockets.

I bought myself a Mars Bar in Woolworth's when we went past. I asked her if she wanted one – I didn't know if veggies could eat them or not. She didn't feel like one, anyway. I did – I comfort-eat when I'm tense.

We crossed the High Street by the Multiscreen and started off aimlessly down The Boulevard when Chloe suddenly had an idea.

'I want to go in the library,' she announced. 'I've got my ticket. I won't be long.'

Once inside, she headed straight for the non-fiction section and started flicking through various tomes on human reproduction and baby-care.

I was heartily embarrassed. 'What if someone *sees* us?' I whispered.

'It's a free country,' she said. 'Anyway, I borrow picture books all the time to paint from.'

I still felt awkward. She eventually took out one with a lot of colour pictures, and stuffed it mercifully out of sight into her bag.

I couldn't wait to get out of there, but she paused by the notice-board in the lobby. I wasn't sure what had grabbed her eye to start with. She rummaged around for a pen and a scrap of paper, and started to copy down some telephone numbers. Pregnancy Crisis Line; Women's Clinic (free advice, no appointment necessary); Haven House (twenty-four-hour helpline).

'You're never going to *ring* these, Clo!' I gasped. 'Not from *home*, surely?'

'I might,' she said dismissively. 'I've got to think things through. I might need to talk to someone who *knows* what they're talking about.' With that, she gave me a pointed look.

'Come *on!*' I said, urgently. 'People might see what you're doing.'

'I could be thinking of taking evening classes. Basket-making. Conversational Japanese,' she replied, evenly. Then she noticed another poster.

'Look!' she said, gesturing at a small handbill. It advertised a public lecture about abortion – the pros and cons – with a speaker whose name meant nothing to me. Plus a film presentation. Admission free (retiring collection in aid of some charity) – all welcome. Tonight. North Green Community Church Centre, 7.45 pm.

'I might as well go,' she said. 'Hattie's out – I've nothing better to do.'

'But North Green's miles away,' I objected.

'It's on a bus route,' she replied.

'Someone might *see* you,' I said, panicking on her behalf.

'I can go if I want to. Going to a meeting doesn't mean I'm saying to the world, "Hey, everybody – I'm preggie!" It's a free country.'

'Keep your voice down,' I croaked. What can you do with someone like that? I steered her outside again, wondering why *I* was the one feeling guilty.

'OK, Clo,' I said. 'Ring the abortion line. *They'll* talk some sense into you – you're obviously not going to listen to me.'

'Shut up, Claire Rayner,' she said.

'Oh, come *on* – what options have you got?'

'That's what I want to find out,' she snapped, blushing and gripping her bag very tightly.

That made me really cross. 'Have it your own way,' I said.

'I intend to! It's *my* problem. You just stop bullying me,' she replied, pinking up around the eyes again. And then she stomped off down The Boulevard.

I stood and watched her go; sometimes best friends can feel like worst enemies.

'She's wrong about one thing,' I thought bitterly. 'How can it be *her* problem when she's just dumped it into my lap without a by-your-leave, and ruined my life with it?'

I was a nervous wreck, for heaven's sake. Couldn't she see what effect it was having on me? She disappeared around the corner by the fire station.

'Probably not,' I decided.

9

Options

I was at the cinema with Oliver. He had his arm around me, and we were watching Gérard Depardieu in a French film – but the funny thing was that it was in English with French subtitles. It was getting ruder and ruder, and I was feeling distinctly uncomfortable watching it with someone else.

Then I realised whose head it was partially blocking my view.

Bruno Villebonne was sprawling in the seat in front, an arm around each of the girls beside him. He turned and smiled at me, and I saw that the two girls were Chloe and Roo. They turned and smiled, too, and lifted up their hands; they were both wearing wedding-rings.

I sat bolt upright in bed, sweating. My nightdress was sticking to my spine, and my heart was pounding. It took a second or two before I realised it wasn't real – you know how vivid dreams can be just before you wake up.

I could tell it wasn't night because of the half-light; I fumbled for the clock. 5.30 am.

Too early to get up. I grabbed a magazine and began

to read the serial to take my mind off things. I must have been really tired, though, because I dozed off again and slid back into crazy, disturbing, Technicolor dreams.

Here was Miss Shue drifting towards me, smiling and saying, 'Don't worry – it's not your responsibility. Just leave it all to me . . . . Here's what you have to do.'

I felt incredible relief. And then I saw Chloe, hugely pregnant like some whale, pushing a pram with twins in it through the park. The whole school was lined up on the grass, shouting insults, laughing and making fun of her.

Mrs P was in the sandpit, crying.

Then she turned into Chloe. I could hear her sobs; they sounded very real. I woke up and realised it was me. *I* was crying.

And that was what it was like after Chloe had broken her news – a nightmare from which I couldn't escape. There was nobody I could tell, no way to get it out of my system. It was a massive, heavy secret I had to lug around like a tonne weight, which was all the more difficult because of the celebrations that followed the coming-out of the results. There was no way I could just sink without trace.

I should have rung Chloe. I know I should have; I was desperate to speak to her. But I couldn't swallow my pride. I kept blaming her for our row, and then I'd blame myself. I was really upset. Added to that, it was one of those weekends when the possibility of having a private telephone conversation was a non-starter; the house was *full* of people.

So I put on a breathtaking performance – RADA, eat your heart out! I was bright, witty, normal (perhaps a bit *too* normal). No-one could tell that I was gutted. Absolutely *gutted*.

First came the family meal at Percy's Brasserie, which ended abruptly when JG flicked ice-cream at the waiter. He's a good shot – I'll say that for him. Then there was a long, long, *long* weekend with Nanna Millie, Gran Sampson and Great-Aunt Ruby coming to stay. Which involved Kate in with me again and JG in a tent in the garden. Best place for him, I say; I wish he'd have stayed there.

Gran Sampson is deaf, Nanna Millie talks about operations all the time – especially during meals – and G-A Ruby doesn't get on with either of them. So it was a laugh-a-minute.

'Why did you invite the Three Stooges all together?' I heard Dad ask Mum in a desperate undertone at one point.

'It wasn't me, it was *you*. Don't you remember?' asked Mum, weakly.

There was a kind of corporate sigh. Then they turned, switched on glossy smiles and strode back into the lounge to take orders for cups of tea and coffee.

Cass rang sometime that weekend to invite me to a party Gregor Lumb was throwing at his house. It emerged that he'd asked her out a few days before, and he was 'quite nice really'. Her dad would give me a lift there and back.

'Shall I ring Clo?' I asked.

Deadly silence.

'Look, Sophe – I *know* you do everything together, but Greg wasn't going to invite her.'

Cass sounded desperately embarrassed. 'The thing is . . . with it being an after-exams party and everything, we thought . . . well, with her getting all A's and that . . . we thought it would put a kind of damper on things. And it's not like he really knows her, anyway.'

She paused for breath. 'I mean, *we're* just average mortals. You know what I mean?'

I did. Normally, I'd have been green with envy about Chloe's results, but just now there were so many other things to worry about that it was way down my panic-list, and I hadn't got that far yet.

'I don't do *everything* with Chloe,' I said, in what I hoped sounded an independent voice. 'Tell Greg thanks – and I'd love to come.'

Actually, it was a rotten party. Cass and her dad called for me in the middle of a classic row between G-A Ruby and Nanna Millie. The G-A was accusing her of stealing her pink bedsocks – for what purpose was unclear. Dad was trying to arbitrate, and the doorbell rang just as the socks were discovered in the G-A's handbag.

'Saved by the bell!' I said, sliding into the car beside Cass.

I'd never been to the Lumbs' house before. They had a superb long garden with a shed ('gazebo') at the end of it – perfect for summer parties. Around it I was relentlessly pursued by a mountainous mutant jellyfish by the name of Andrew, who couldn't get it into his skull that I didn't find blubber appealing.

Cass was tied up – literally – with Greg all evening, and there was a conspicuous lack of singles. Hence the persistence of the Incredible Hulk. Hugh and Gill turned up later, and although I thought I'd got over him, seeing them together like that rankled. Well, to be honest, *everything* was rankling at that party.

So I spent most of my time hiding in a corner, watching Phil Banks spike Mr Lumb's punch with Sainsbury's vodka. There was only one good thing about the whole evening: At least it was easy to spot Andrew approaching. I tell you, that guy made Pavarotti look anorexic.

I'd hoped a change of scene would take me out of myself, but it wasn't any good. I got more and more depressed, longing for the moment when Cass's dad would arrive and take us home. And, of course, Cass was the *last* to leave.

However, I came to one important conclusion while I wallowed in misery: I'd been rotten to Clo. I'd been so absorbed by my own feelings that I'd ignored *hers*. Instead of being supportive and providing a listening ear like friends are supposed to do, I'd just been irritable and ratty and picked arguments with her. And all that at a time when she needed a shoulder to cry on more than ever before.

I took a deep swig from my Coke can, and suddenly spat it out all over the sofa when I realised some idiot had put a fag-end in it. Gross. Honestly – some *people*.

A*nd* I felt guilty coming to a party that Clo hadn't been invited to; guilty and disloyal. I decided to ring her as soon as I could and apologise.

It wasn't all philanthropy, though; I was desperate to talk and talk and talk, and she was the only person I could talk *to*. You can't bottle things up for ever.

When I got home that evening, I was over-tired and overwrought. Kate was dead to the world, snoring in a funny little-girl way, with her legs and arms all over the place. I didn't want to go to bed because I was afraid of having nightmares. All I could think of was Chloe.

OK, so getting pregnant isn't the end of the world, but nobody could have convinced me of that *then*. Time was running out; school started in a couple of weeks. Whatever she did, it would have to be *fast*.

I started to cry, very quietly, snuffling into my pillow. I knew I would get a yelling-at in the morning because my mascara was running all over it, but I didn't care. My emotions were in tatters; too much had happened too quickly, and I felt incapable of dealing with it. I even prayed – that's how miserable I was.

'God,' I muttered, feeling stupid. 'if you're up there, can't you get Clo out of this mess and magic everything back to how it was before?'

As *if*. This was real life, and I knew it; and fairy tales *don't* come true. But I felt better for having done it – so much so that I fell asleep. And I didn't have bad dreams. In fact, I overslept.

Monday dawned bright and fair, but with a tiny hint of September in it – a smell of fallen leaves and distant bonfires and a new, sudden chill in the wind. One of those days when you somehow *know* that summer's grinding to a halt, and that school can only be just around the corner.

Whatever *else* might lie around that corner, I couldn't bear to think.

Chloe, though, has always been a thinker. She'd been working things out and was about to shock me again. What she'd actually *done* was something I'd never have imagined. Not of Clo.

I kept putting off phoning her. First I got engrossed in *Going Live*. Then I started reading a magazine. Then something else happened – you know how it is when there's something you're trying to avoid doing. I wanted to see her, but I *hate* having to say sorry. My apology was sticking in my throat like a lump of mouldy tofu (whatever that was).

In the end, *she* rang *me*.

I was surprised she was still speaking to me.

'Sophe, can you come over?' she asked. She didn't sound offended or anything. 'Mum's busy – you can stay for lunch. There's a lentil roast – real food, this time.'

'Sure,' I said dubiously, trying to work out what mood she was in. I'd wait until I saw her to apologise, I decided, because there was something in her manner I couldn't fathom. She still didn't sound quite right.

'Is everything OK?' I asked gingerly.

'It's settled,' she said. 'I've made my mind up. I'll tell you about it when you come around.'

'What *now*?' I wondered to myself morosely, putting the receiver down. She sounded so *definite* that I was afraid for one moment that she'd decided to commit suicide or something.

As I trudged over to her place, I rehearsed my words of contrition in a million different ways, each suitable for a different Chloe-mood.

It was while I rang her bell that it suddenly dawned on me what it was that had puzzled me when she phoned. She hadn't sounded as I'd expected, because she was back to *normal*.

It was the *old* Chloe Prentice I'd been speaking to.

10

No options

'This is nice,' I said.

(Play it cool, Sophe. Keep the conversation very basic until you can work out what's going on.)

'Yes,' said Chloe. 'It's Soukous from Zaïre. Jolly, isn't it?'

'Yeah, jolly,' I repeated, listening to the track. It was a catchy number with an insistent, dance-like rhythm and not the sort of thing a depressed person would be listening to.

(Come on Chloe, give me some clue: what's up?)

'Coffee or tea? We've got Earl Grey, Lapsang Souchong, Green Gunpowder or that herbal whatsit – red thingy. *You* know – Hattie gave you some once.'

Oh, *that*. Dishwater and hibiscus, I think it was.

'I'll have the one with the most caffeine in it,' I said.

Chloe giggled. 'You're in the wrong house, then . . . .'

I was starting to relax; somehow, it was like old times again. I was thinking madly.

(Tell me, Chloe, what's happened? You aren't *supposed* to be happy! Don't say *you've* been happy all weekend while I'*ve* been growing ulcers. What gives?)

'I wanted to apologise, Sophe,' she said, giving me one of her direct, challenging stares and hooking her hair behind her left ear. She was wearing her Chinese pottery earrings, the pair that don't match.

'Apologise?' I began.

She apologise to *me?* Oh, well, if that was how she wanted it, who was *I* to complain?

'Yes,' she continued. 'I've been a right pain. I know I've had a good excuse and everything, but I've been pretty bad company.'

(She could say that again!)

'I just wanted to say sorry. I had no right to dump my problems on you and get ratty. It must have upset *you*, too – I kept forgetting that.'

'Yeah, it did,' I mumbled. 'Look, I'm sorry, too – it takes two to fight, you know. I haven't been a barrel of laughs myself. Shake on it?'

And we solemnly shook hands, a ritual we'd carried out every time we'd quarrelled since we were six years old and in pigtails.

'This'll sound stupid,' I said, 'but I've sort of missed you. Since the disco. We've let things drive us apart just when we needed each other.'

'That goes for me, too.'

'What's happened?'

'A lot,' said Chloe, still looking straight at me. Sometimes I can stare her out; sometimes we make games of it. Today I couldn't. In fact, for a second I almost didn't recognise her; there was something in her that shocked me once I'd put my finger on it, because it was so unexpected. She was *excited* – you could feel it. Almost touch it.

No, that's not explaining it well – she was *bubbly*, like when you're a kid and waiting to be taken to a birthday party. There was lightheartedness and confidence and fun mixed up in it. *Fun*, for goodness' sake – at a time like *this?*

I was confused, and cast around for explanations. 'She's hysterical. She's been at Mrs P's gin. She's gone mad. Stark raving bananas.'

I waited for her to make the first move.

'Sophie,' she said, 'I *know* what I'm going to do.'

My eyes must have flickered suspiciously, because she hurried on.

'It's all right. I know. I just *know*. I'm going to have the baby, and everything's going to be all right!'

'Your mother *is* out, isn't she? Have you told her yet?' I asked, struck by a fleeting doubt.

'No – and no. She's got a day off. She's on the patio doing something to her geraniums – she won't hear us with all this ethnic stuff on. Why?'

'Chlo-eee! You . . . you . . . Dumbo!' The girl was hopeless. 'Look,' I said, 'if we talk – we talk *upstairs*. OK? For the sake of my nerves.'

'OK,' said Clo, and we trooped up to her room. As I stumped up the stairs behind her, I decided it had to be Bruno. He'd proposed. Must have – nothing else could explain the change in her.

I made sure the door and window were firmly shut before I let her open her mouth again.

'Now, then,' I demanded, 'what's all this about?'

'Everything's changed. I've got a lot to tell you, but let me do it *my* way. Just *listen*.'

I could see from her eyes that she meant it, so I shut up. She settled herself down comfortably on the bed and crossed her legs before continuing.

'I'd better start at the beginning. I've been doing some research, and it's made me think very hard.' She fished around under her pillow.

'That's one of the reasons I wanted to see you,' she went on, with her I'm-about-to-deliver-a-lecture face. 'You've lied to me and tried to bully me, and I won't fall for it and I don't want *you* to fall for it any longer, either.'

'What are you on about? Lied? Bullied? *Me?*'

'You heard.'

'You explain that, Chloe Prentice!' I stuttered.

'I intend to,' she said simply. And that was the odd thing; I realised then that she wasn't angry. Not a bit. She was detached, matter-of-fact. It was impossible for me to stay cross with her when she was like that.

'Look, I didn't mean to get at you,' she said with a sigh, 'but the thing is, Sophe, you're the best friend I've ever had, and I've got to set things straight. This is *important*. You'll just listen – promise?'

I nodded. 'I've never been the depressive type, but I've really let things get on top of me recently,' she went on. 'I felt as if everyone was persecuting me, pressurising me. I needed space to think, and nobody was giving me straight answers. *You* certainly weren't.'

I kept quiet. Well, I'd promised.

'I've never been convinced about abortion, but I wasn't clear in my own mind *why*. I wanted facts. You know, something I could tell the doctor when I go back this week, something that would sound *sensible*. And now I know.'

I noticed that she was holding some booklets in her hand that she'd pulled out from beneath her pillow.

'I'm not blaming you, Sophie; really I'm not. You're just saying things you've been told. But the thing is, you haven't *thought* about it. You just believe what everyone wants you to believe.'

She passed me the booklets; they were about abortion.

'This is what I found out. I want you to read these; *you* were the one talking about tonsils and tadpoles. It was a pack of lies, and I'm not letting you get away with it.'

I couldn't get angry, because Chloe had a point. I *didn't* know what I really thought because I'd never bothered to find out.

'OK,' I said, and went to tuck them in my jeans pocket. Chloe grabbed my wrist.

'No,' she said. '*Now*.'

'Look, we *did* all this in biology,' I protested.

Chloe glared at me. 'Yes, we were *supposed* to have done it, but you obviously didn't listen to anything you were told because you don't know it *now*,' she said.

OK, I admit it; she was right. I thought back to the sex education film Wiggie had shown us, and how I'd spent the whole time messing about on the back row, only watching when the gory or rude bits came on. Well, it was a stupid film, except for the male model with the impressive tackle. Embarrassingly soppy music and a patronising voice-over. Cringe material.

However, there's no arguing with Clo when she goes all militant. She looked positively ferocious. So I began, with some misgivings, to read. The enormity of what I read is still with me. I think Chloe achieved something no-one had ever managed before – she made me think, *really* think. And I've been doing a lot of that lately.

The first booklet was called A *Few Things You Didn't Know about Yourself*. It had a colour picture of an unborn baby on it. He was very beautiful – you could see fine veins running just under the skin; you could even see his eyelashes.

'This child is eighteen weeks old from the point of conception', ran the caption. I steeled myself, because I was sure it was all going to be heart-tugging stuff. I didn't know the half of it. The inside of the leaflet was divided into paragraphs, each with an accompanying diagram of an unborn baby, a foetus. I caught Chloe's eye, and began to read.

What were you doing before you were born?

Day 1

Your father's sperm has met your mother's ovum and fertilised it. Everything about you is determined at that point: your gender, build, personality, eye- and hair-colour. You start your journey towards your mother's womb, stopping her menstrual cycle and triggering off in her all those changes needed to help you develop. A unique person has begun to live.

Day 20

You have developed your own blood cells and established a placenta (afterbirth). The rudiments of your nervous system appear. Your mother has just missed her first menstrual period.

Day 30

Your heart has formed and has started to beat. You are about 0.5 cm (¼ inch) long, but already your brain has grown to human proportions. You have rudimentary eyes, mouth, ears, a spine and nervous system. Your mother probably still doesn't know she's carrying you.

Day 56

You are over 2 cm (1 inch) long. All your major internal organs are present and functioning –

they only need time to mature. Your skeleton is complete in cartilage. Reflexes are present and electrical brain-wave activity is measurable. You discover that you can wiggle your spine. Your mother has only just missed her second period.

I paused, gasping at the thought of how well formed a foetus could be at such a young age.

Week 10

You discover how to make a fist, and can grasp an object that is touching your palm. You work out how to jump up and down and co-ordinate your movements. You are 4 cm (nearly 2 inches) long.

Week 11

You are completely formed and look much as you will on the day you'll be born – only tinier. You are as long as a little finger and have become very active, although your mother can't feel you yet. You have found out how to do somersaults, and when your mother moves, you move, too, in order to find a comfortable position. You realise that you can make facial expressions.

Week 16

You recognise and respond to your mother's voice, and can distinguish between her and another woman reading the same story. Your sex is clearly obvious. You like listening to outside sounds, and can even recognise the theme music of your mother's favourite TV programmes. You develop a taste for music – you kick gently to the sound of classical music, whereas rock makes you kick fast. Your mother still doesn't really look pregnant.

'I wonder what he'll think of Hattie's ethnic reggae?' I wondered silently, smiling weakly at Chloe, who was watching me intently.

Week 20

The hair on your head begins to grow. You are 25 cm (10 inches) long and fully active because you still have plenty of room. Against all odds, some babies born prematurely at the age you are now have survived, given specialist medical care.

Week 24

You move around vigorously, and sometimes play games with your mother, kicking back if she presses her tummy. She will probably need to start wearing maternity clothes now. You are said to be 'viable' – mature enough to sustain an independent existence outside your mother's body if born now. From this point on, you are safe. Up until now, she could – at any point – have legally chosen to have you killed.

Week 28

Your eyes are open and you recognise light, which you can see filtering through your mother's tummy in the same way as a torch-beam shines through fingers. If she sunbathes, you will move around excitedly. The longer you stay within her womb, the bigger and stronger you will be.

Week 40

You are born. Congratulations; you're one of the survivors.

I put the booklet down carefully, trying to take it all in; this was no tadpole we were talking about. I glanced up at Chloe, who was impatiently waiting for me to finish reading.

'I want you to realise,' she said, 'that I'm ten weeks pregnant. Ten, ten-and-a-half – something like that. Think about it! My baby looks like . . . that one.'

She stabbed a finger at one of the illustrations.

'Complete. Full nervous system and all that. Look; he's this big.'

She held up her little finger.

'That big, and perfect. Tiny and perfect. A baby baby. That's fantastic, isn't it?' Her eyes were shining. 'He's moving and kicking, even though I can't feel him.'

I just stared at her stomach, which was as flat as ever. No sign of anything. It seemed almost unbelievable at that moment that this could actually be happening – I suppose part of me still hoped we were in some dream we'd wake up from sooner or later.

'Go on,' she insisted. 'There's more.'

I picked up the next leaflet, which was in the form of a small book without illustrations. It was called *In the Dark*.

What you *won't* be told about abortion

You wouldn't marry someone without having got to know them first. It wouldn't be sensible to buy a pair of shoes if you hadn't tried them on. And you certainly wouldn't buy a used car if you didn't know anything about its history, would you?

In life, when you have a choice to make, you find out all the facts beforehand to help you reach a decision. Because the consequences of that decision have to be lived with, you don't want to make a mistake.

It's the same with abortion. Without the full facts, how can you make an informed choice? And yet the things you need to know are the very things your medical advisers are unlikely to tell you.

Three things you should know about abortion

1. What happens before abortion?

You probably won't be told you're carrying a *baby* – he'll be called something impersonal like a product of conception, a foetus or tissue.

I swallowed hard, guilt overwhelming me. My theory about tonsils and tadpoles seemed *ridiculous* in the light of this.

But he *is* a baby, and he's been alive from the moment he was conceived. He's his own person. He's not part of *you*.

By the time you realised you were pregnant, your baby was almost fully formed and looked like a full-term infant – only smaller. The only differences between him and a newborn baby are his size and the fact that he's too immature to live apart from you right now.

He can squint, swallow, turn somersaults, have the hiccups and suck his thumb. All his organs are functioning, and he can feel pain.

2. What happens during abortion?

Everyone has felt revulsion about the cruelty meted out to laboratory animals – you might even have boycotted firms involved in animal experimentation.

'Or, if you were Chloe's mum, you'd be organising protest marches,' I thought.

But you probably won't have been told about what happens to human babies during the abortion process.

Methods of abortion have to be extremely powerful, as the developing infant is surprisingly strong. This carries inevitable risks for the mother and her future ability to have children.

For all but the earliest abortions (which are usually performed using general anaesthetic), the mother is conscious during a full labour, at the end of which she will give birth to a dead child. This is a lengthy and distressing process, particularly if she hasn't been prepared for what will happen or told that she might see her baby.

Women who have undergone such terminations frequently describe the experience as 'horrific'; the emotional cost to the mother is considerable. The cost to the child is his right to live.

A baby's nervous system develops very early on during the pregnancy; we know that the child who dies by abortion dies in pain.

There are several different methods of terminating a pregnancy, depending on the age of the child. These are:

Up to about 12 weeks

D & C A curette, a type of knife, is inserted into the womb. The baby is cut up and scraped out.

'Read on,' Chloe said, noticing my shocked face and guessing where I'd got to. 'You need to know the *truth*.'

Vacuum aspiration A tube is inserted into the womb and connected to a suction pump. The baby is torn apart and sucked into a jar.

These two methods are performed under general anaesthetic.

Prostaglandin termination Premature labour is induced through administering this hormone by pessary or injection. The mother experiences strong contractions and is conscious throughout labour, finally giving birth to a dead baby. Contractions can be strong enough to dismember the infant. Afterwards, she will need an operation to scrape out her womb and ensure that nothing has been left behind to set up infection.

Yuk!

RU486 This new method, which is at present only allowed in the UK and France, induces miscarriage through medical rather than surgical means. The mother takes a series of tablets, then goes into a 'mini-labour' and delivers a dead child. The whole process takes several days and its success-rate is not a hundred per cent.

Over about 12 weeks

Prostaglandin termination This method is used for larger babies in the same way as in early pregnancy.

Hysterotomy (not the same as hysterectomy) This method is basically Caesarean section, where an incision is made into the abdomen and the baby

removed. In this case, though, he will be just left to die.

'Murderers!' I thought savagely. 'How *could* they?' Then I realised that I was beginning to take Chloe's side. Regaining control, I read on.

In the next ward a mother could be giving birth to a premature baby of the same age; unlike the aborted baby, he will be whisked into an incubator and everything possible done to ensure his survival.

D & C and hysterotomy are now infrequently used in the UK because of the associated dangers for the mother.

3. What happens after the abortion?

All surgical procedures have risks, and those of abortion are seriously underestimated. Abortion is a major factor in the death-rate of pregnant women.

Around one in ten women who have had a termination will suffer complications of some type. These can include bleeding, infection, damage to the cervix and rupture of the womb.

'Having an abortion is only like having your tonsils out.' Did I *really* say those words to Chloe?

Women who have had abortions may experience problems in future pregnancies. Rates for miscarriage, premature delivery, low birth-weight babies, prolonged labour and sterility are much higher than for women who have never had a termination; there may also be difficulty in

conceiving in the first place. The infant mortality rate is also higher for mothers who have had a termination in the past.

Most women will suffer from some degree of emotional stress following abortion, sometimes immediately and sometimes after a lapse of time. Abortion is a form of bereavement, and to come to terms with it, grieving needs to take place.

If this is not allowed to happen, the result can be a lifetime of guilt, remorse and nightmares. For some women, the emotional stress can reach intense levels and embrace symptoms such as depression, alcoholism, personality change, eating disorders or drug addiction.

What happens now?

If you are contemplating abortion, don't rush into it. *You* are the one who will have to live with the consequences of your decision – don't make that decision until you have fully considered what's involved.

Don't let anyone push you into something you aren't sure about – remember, *no-one* can take away your baby without your consent.

Abortion is *never* the only way out. Organisations exist to support you in your choice to keep your baby; telephone the number overleaf for confidential free counselling and help.

Your pregnancy may be unwanted, but there is no such thing as an unwanted baby.

On the back page there was a printed empty box, in which someone had wonkily rubber-stamped the telephone number of a help-line. There was also an address and the names 'Mac and Tilly' scribbled in felt-tip above it.

My head was swimming. Chloe handed me the last leaflet, a thin fold of paper with a joky drawing on the front, showing a girl scratching her head. In a bubble she was asking, 'Crisis? What crisis?'

Are you pregnant and don't want to be? Are you scared? Confused? Under pressure to have an abortion?

Don't feel as if there's no-one to talk to and nowhere you can turn. There *is*.

We can offer you free, confidential pregnancy testing and counselling – no appointment necessary.

Ring us or call in – we'll help.

Underneath was the address, telephone number and opening times of The Haven Centre, Station Road, North Green.

I laid down the booklets on the bedspread with exaggerated care and stared at them. If you open your eyes very wide and don't blink, sometimes you can stop yourself crying.

I felt choked. It took time for me to get my vocal cords under control. Even then, all I could manage was a little squeaky, 'I'm sorry, Clo. I didn't *know*.'

'Yeah, I realise that.'

She glanced away, and then rose and went over to the window. From there she'd be looking out over the tangly patch of garden, over the patio with its ancient deckchairs and its terracotta pots overflowing with geraniums. If Mrs P hadn't dug them all up by now, that is.

But I could also tell that Chloe was looking without really seeing. I think she was doing that because she didn't want to look me in the eyes when she said her next words.

11

Present . . . tense

'Sophie, I'm leaving.'

'You *what*?'

'I'll be going away. Leaving. *You* know.'

Chloe still had her back to me, and that didn't tell me much about how she was feeling. I could see her shoulders hunched and her hands digging deeply into her pockets.

My ears had heard what she'd said, but the words hadn't reached my brain yet.

'I'm going to Morton Green. There's a good tech there – I can transfer to it for my A-levels. I could do them in two years, or three. The baby's due in March, so it's difficult to plan, really – we'll just have to see how it goes. After that, I'd like to go on to art college, if I can . . . .'

Her voice tailed off, projected into an invisible future.

'What are you saying?'

She opened the window one notch and the breeze lifted her hair a little, bringing into the room the scent of flowers. She turned to me again and pushed her hands even deeper into her jeans. I noticed again that energy about her. She stayed by the window but kept her voice low.

'You know that meeting we saw advertised at the library?'

I nodded.

'Well, I went. It was over at North Green, in the Community Church Centre. I sat at the back; I didn't know what to expect. Anyway, there was some hymn-singing and then the speaker came on. She talked about abortion, all the facts and everything, and honestly, Sophe, it made sense. It was exactly what I'd been wanting to find out. As she spoke, it kind of fell into place what I should do. I can't explain it any better than that. Do you know what I mean?'

I didn't, but I nodded anyway.

'Then they showed a video – you've read the leaflets. They pretty much sum up what it was about. She warned us it would be disturbing, and she was right. I was in tears, Sophe, I really was. They showed an early abortion being done, and you could actually *see* the baby scream as it was being cut up.'

She sounded as if she had a lump in her throat, and she stopped for a moment. 'How can they do that? How can anyone do it?'

I shuddered involuntarily.

Chloe heaved a great sigh before going on. 'That's not all,' she said. 'The woman spoke again after the video, and it was just the weirdest thing. It was as if she was speaking directly to *me*. Then, at the end, she said, "There's a girl here who's discovered she's pregnant and doesn't know where to turn. She's feeling pressurised to have a termination, but she wants to have the baby. Whoever you are, I want to pray for you. Come and see me afterwards." '

'Coincidence,' I thought but didn't say. 'Religious nuts. Fruit-cakes.'

Chloe was watching me intently.

'It was *me*, Sophie; I swear it. I felt hot and shaky all over. I couldn't wait for the meeting to end. There were a few people chatting at the front, but I just *had* to wait to speak to her. When she'd finished, she just looked at me and said, "It's you, isn't it?" I said, "Yes." Then this married couple came over, and we all went out the back. I told them everything.'

'You told *strangers* . . . ?' I broke in.

'Yeah, but it wasn't like that,' Chloe said, passionately. 'I just *had* to. Anyway, it was as if they already *knew*. They were like people I'd always known. Oh, I don't know how to put it!'

She tossed her hair back and thought about it a bit more.

'It felt . . . exciting, like something was about to happen. Look, I can't put it any better. Am I making sense?'

No.

'Er – yes,' I said politely.

'Judith – that was the speaker – said I needed God. She said that, without him, there was a huge hole in my life that would never be filled and that I had to invite Jesus into my life.'

She stopped when she saw my face.

'It made *sense*, Sophe. It was *real!* You know me – the school prayer is about as religious as I've ever got. I hadn't a clue what she was on about. I just knew she was *right*.

' "Jesus is a real person," Judith said. "Just talk to him like he's here." So I did. And oh, Sophie! I just . . . it was just . . . wham! I was flattened. Honestly. *Literally*. There was like this tidal wave of power, or something, or joy – I don't know. I went all limp and I'd have fallen over it I hadn't been sitting down. I just sat there *laughing*. For ages! I felt incredible. Clean. So . . . so *happy!*'

She was still feeling it, whatever on earth 'it' was. You could tell. Then her brow clouded, and she looked at me.

'Are you following all this?' she asked.

I felt deeply confused. I was reluctant to say what I really thought – it would have sounded rude. But we'd always been honest with each other, Clo and me.

'I don't know, Clo,' I said dubiously. 'It sounds peculiar. Weird. Who *are* these people?'

'Christians – you know, born-again ones. North Green Community Church.'

'Never heard of it. What is it? Some weirdo sect? It's not that . . . *brainwashing*, is it?'

Then I shut up. I saw her face.

'Oh, do me a favour, will you? Be happy for me, OK?'

I'd try. I'd really try.

'So,' I said, trying – to sound casual, 'what did you mean about going away?'

She settled herself back on the bed again. 'That's part of it,' she said. 'The church is involved with a charity called The Haven; they provide support for girls who want to have their babies. That means accommodation. They say they can put me up with a family and I can go to college until the baby's born.'

'What *then?*' I asked.

'I've thought about this really carefully – please don't think I haven't. And it's my own decision – nobody's pushed me into anything. I want the baby to be adopted. Part of me wants to keep him, but what future could I give a child? How could I support him? What kind of life could I give us? It's not because I'm putting my career before my child.'

My *child*. How odd that sounded.

'I . . . I'm just thinking about what's best for him. I suppose it's partly because I've known Tony and Ruth for so long and I've seen what they went through before they adopted the twins, and I've seen the loving home they've given them.'

She shifted to a more comfortable position before continuing.

'There's just no question in my mind. I'm *sure* about it. That's not to say it's going to be easy, though. I'm terrified. I don't honestly know if I'm going to have the guts to do it when the time comes. I just *know* it's what's going to be right for me. Us,' she finished up, breathlessly.

I *know* . . . I'm *sure* . . . . Although Chloe had in the past always *appeared* definite about what she believed, I could see it for what it was – a front, a pretence. Now her certainty was different; this was the genuine article. I found it disconcerting in the extreme.

It was then that the fact that my best friend was going away began to sink in. Going away literally and metaphorically, because I felt as if she'd suddenly turned into an alien. And my fluency in Martian is a bit rusty. I was floundering about, trying to tune in to a wavelength I could communicate with her on, and failing. Utterly.

'So, why do you have to go to Morton Green? Why can't you stay here?' I asked, desperately.

'Oh, Sophie, I can't. I just *can't*. I couldn't bear everyone to know and gossip about me. It'd be humiliating. You know how people are. You can't ask me to go through that – you just *can't*.'

'What about your mum? She might not let you go. You're not over eighteen yet, you know.'

'I'll talk her round. It'd be easier on her, too, if I wasn't here. Anyway, she's not the broody, gooey-over-babies type, is she? Don't you think?'

'But you can't just go off with people you don't know! You only met them on Friday. You don't *know* them. You're being a bit hasty, aren't you?'

'Look, I've got no choice. Term starts soon and if I'm going to make the break it'll have to be *now*. Anyway, you haven't met them and I *have* – they're a great crowd. I spent a lot of time with them over the weekend – Mac and Tilly invited me over on Saturday afternoon, and I went to lunch with Donald and Bron after church on Sunday.'

'Who *are* all these people?'

'Mac and Tilly are the couple who prayed with me after the meeting. Mid-twenties, married, no kids; he's a trainee accountant. She's a secretary.'

'And Donald?'

'He's the pastor – vicar, minister, whatever – of the church. Bron's his wife. Four kids, huge messy house, loads of laughs. They'd invited another couple to lunch, too – John and Fiona. They're from Morton Green, and it's them I'll be living with until I have the baby. Their house is near the college. They're really nice.'

Typical Chloe. She'd got it all worked out down to the fine details. Just shows what *chutzpah* can do for you.

'What on earth have you been telling your mother? How have you explained your amazing mood-changes?' I demanded.

'Nerves over the results, mostly. She hasn't said anything. But then, she's had a lot of hassle herself lately. She's had to do a lot of extra nights on the Women's Refuge phone-line with the holidays, and then there was the other business. You'll have read about it in the paper.'

'No, I haven't.'

'A woman came to the Refuge a while back. Battered wife; really disturbed. They were going to have to find her somewhere else to go because she was making a lot of trouble for the other residents, but before they did she committed suicide. They found her hanging in the ladies'. She used a pair of tights. The Refuge has had a lot of criticism because of it – I don't think Hattie's had many spare brain-cells left over to spend on anything else recently.'

'It wasn't Hattie who found . . . .'

'No, thank goodness – she'd have freaked. It was Josie who found her – pretty awful for them all, though. Hattie's very cut up.'

'What did she say when you told her you were going to church?'

'Bit surprised. Didn't say a lot, really. I think she was pleased I'd got some new friends – she reckons I've been staying in too much recently. I hope she likes them.'

'Likes them?'

'Yes – Donald and Bron are going to have us both round for a meal once she knows. It may seem like I'm doing all this behind her back, but before I tell her I've got to make sure everything's one hundred per cent organised and that it's all going to work out.'

Chloe hoisted up her legs and crossed them again. 'Won't be able to do this for much longer!' she said.

'I wish you didn't have to go,' I said.

'Yeah,' said Chloe. 'There's a lot of things I wish. But I've got to say it: This is like a dream come true for me. I can't believe it's really happening. I feel so *good*, and the people from the church are so *nice* – really caring. Genuine. I feel as if I've found my long-lost family and I'm coming home at last.'

I was trying to be happy for her, but I couldn't quite get there. I was *losing* her. She'd got new friends, a new life; I could feel her slipping away. I know it wasn't intentional, but she seemed to be forgetting me already. She was forging ahead into the future, just like she'd always done.

The anxieties I'd been tortured by began to give way to sadness and a general unease.

'But, Clo,' I broke in, 'why should you go through all that and have a baby for someone else? No-one can expect you to do that!'

She looked at me sadly. 'You still don't get it, do you?' she said. 'I already *have* the baby. Nothing's going to change *that*. The question is, whether I kill him or not.'

I sighed. 'So it's all settled, then . . . .'

'All settled.'

'And Bruno?'

'No,' she said hurriedly. 'I can't tell him. I'm not ready. I can't face him, and I can't tell him.'

'I suppose he doesn't have to know.'

'Oh, but he *does!*' said Clo, turning to me, her face flushed. 'That's what Tilly said – and she has a point. He's got the right to know. But there's a lot happening now, and I can't do everything at once. I just need some space. I'll tell him sometime – but I can't do it *now*.'

(Whether she's done it yet, I don't know; the Big B's got enough on his plate at the moment anyway, it would seem. Because we *did* discover later how the ravishing Roo had got him back after their slanging match, and how she managed to get engaged, move to Oxford to be near him and fix a wedding for November. He'd got *her* pregnant, too.)

'Anyway,' pursued Chloe, 'I can't tell *him* if I haven't told Hattie, can I?'

'So,' I said, gullible fool that I am, 'when are you going to tell *her*?'

'Right *now*,' said Clo.

12

Past imperfect

'Chloeee!' I squealed. She couldn't mean it. I was right – she *had* flipped.

'You've flipped!' I said.

'No, I haven't. Come with me.' Chloe grabbed my elbow, but I shook myself free.

'Oh, no. N*o way*. This is private stuff. *I can't*.'

Clo looked me in the eye, and it was like a snake hypnotising its victim – I was lost. I'd *have* to go along with her.

'N*ow?*' I said weakly.

'N*ow*,' said Chloe. 'Before I change my mind.'

She pulled me after her, and that walk down to the kitchen was like a march to the scaffold. But if I felt bad, I reasoned, how on earth must Clo have been feeling?

'Hi, there!' said Mrs P cheerfully over the top of the G*uardian* as we entered the kitchen. 'There's tea in the pot if you want it – I've just made some.'

'Mum, I need to talk to you,' said Chloe.

The smile froze on Mrs Prentice's face, and she slowly lowered her paper.

'Mum – I'm pregnant.'

Talk about being blunt!

The silence went on for ever; nobody said anything. We just stood there, staring at each other and feeling like death.

'Oh, dear God!' said Mrs P, suddenly lunging for her bag and fumbling around in it for her secret cigarettes. She found one, lit it with trembling fingers and took a long, deep drag.

'I *have* given it up,' she said, pointlessly. Then, 'God, I needed that!'

Suddenly she started laughing. It was dreadful. I wanted to be anywhere, anywhere but there. It was a terrible, despairing laugh – there was nothing happy in it.

'I'm sorry,' she said after a minute or two, pulling herself together with some effort. 'It's just that you've dumped on me the very thing every mother dreads.'

She looked at Chloe uncomprehendingly.

Chloe wilted.

'I'd never, never have believed it of *you*, Coco . . . . You *are* sure?'

She took another pull at her Gauloise before running on.

'Of course you're sure. You wouldn't have come to me if you weren't sure. It's funny – I didn't even know you were seeing anyone.'

Then her eyes widened. 'It wasn't Howard?'

'No,' said Chloe.

'Thank heavens for that,' breathed Mrs P. 'I worried about the way he looked at you sometimes. Anyway, he's past history. It was too long ago.'

There was another long pause. I wished she'd get angry or cry or tell Chloe off or something. Anything so you could tell how she was taking it. But you couldn't.

'How far on are you?' she asked at last. She looked up at Chloe, and her eyes were . . . just desolate.

I wanted to die.

'Ten weeks – -ish,' said Chloe.

And then there was another of those transformations when Chloe and her mother seemed to have changed places.

'What are you going to do?' asked Mrs P simply.

'I'm going to have it, of course,' said Clo.

'Thank God for that!'

I suppose you never really know how people will react to bad news until it happens. This was one conversation I'd run and rerun in my mind before the event, wondering how it would go. But it wasn't turning out like any of my possible scenarios. I mean, Mrs P hadn't asked who the father was or anything, or lectured Clo about the Pill.

'What?' Chloe was saying, and I got my ears back in gear.

'You've made the right decision, Coke. That takes real guts.'

Chloe had prepared all her anti-abortion arguments, but it seemed she wasn't going to need them. The wind was taken right out of her sails.

'I didn't think you'd feel this way about it,' Clo admitted, looking carefully at her mother. 'I thought you'd want me to have an abortion – I mean, you're so keen on women's rights.'

'No, no – it's not like that, Clo. I'm pro-life – it's just that we've never talked about it. Perhaps we should've. It's my fault, I know – I've deliberately avoided the subject. I find it . . . very, very hard to talk about. Too emotive.'

'I don't understand. I thought I knew what you believed – I thought all feminists were pro-abortion.'

'Women's rights and human rights aren't always the same

thing, Chloe,' she said, bitterly, lighting another cigarette from the butt of the first. 'What about the human rights of the foetus? Anyway, you don't say *pro-abortion*. No-one's *pro*-abortion. It's called *pro-choice*.'

There was a short silence, as if Mrs P were wondering whether or not to say something else. Then she made up her mind.

'Look,' she said, 'there's something I haven't told you before. I said to myself that I'd never burden you with it, but now I think you've got a right to know. They say confession's good for the soul.'

'I'll go,' I said, glad of a chance to escape. 'This is personal.'

'No, Sophie. You can hear this,' said Mrs P. 'I'd rather you heard it straight from me – Chloe'll tell you, anyway.'

She puffed at her Gauloise, marshalling her thoughts, and looked straight at Chloe.

'I had a termination six years before I had you,' she said at last. 'I was at university and didn't want anyone to know. My doctor said it was the wrong time for me, that it would ruin my career. *What* career, huh? Anyway, he said an abortion would be quite straightforward, and I believed that garbage.

'I was just a student. I wasn't ready for a baby, didn't know the first thing about them, wasn't the maternal type. So I went through with it – it seemed easier. But it was the worst thing I ever did in my life. You can't run away from something like that – it haunts you.'

She stared into the distance through a halo of smoke.

'I was young and I was scared. The only person I told was my boyfriend, and he insisted on the abortion. Afterwards, I blamed him. I said, "You made me do it – you made me do it!", but it was *me* who had to sign the paper.'

Clo caught her mother's eye questioningly.

'No, it wasn't your father,' she said. 'Just someone I knew once – someone I wish I'd never laid eyes on.

'I persuaded myself it was only like having a tooth out. But as soon as I got to the hospital . . . I *knew.* I panicked and told the nurse I'd changed my mind. She said, "It's a bit late for that, now, isn't it, dearie? You can't waste the doctor's time!" I just let everyone push me into it.'

It was hard to visualise Mrs P as young and scared – I couldn't imagine anyone pushing her into anything these days. I listened.

'I came round from the anaesthetic crying for my lost baby. It was sheer hell – I'd have given *anything* to undo what I'd done. I was obsessed with it for months – everywhere I looked there were pregnant women or mums and babies. I suppose it was a kind of breakdown, and I felt I deserved it. I thought God was punishing me for killing my baby.

'I'm convinced it would have been a boy. A tiny, perfect little boy.'

She shook her head, as if to dispel the memory.

'And the worst of it was that I couldn't tell anyone. There was no-one to talk to. No-one to counsel me. *Nothing.* I tell you, Chloe, there isn't one day goes by when I don't think of that baby – he'd have been twenty-two this year. I carry him around with me all the time. I wonder what he'd have looked like, who he'd have been, what sports he'd have liked, whether he'd have enjoyed *Star Wars* – that sort of thing. I'm still grieving for him, longing for him. You can't buck responsibilities like that. They don't go. *Ever.*'

Mrs P fixed Chloe with a hard stare. 'My doctor betrayed my trust when I was in no fit state to make a decision.

I was confused, vulnerable, desperate. I was ill – throwing up all over the place. Being in digs, it was a nightmare trying to hide it.

'It was rush, rush, rush all the way. Nobody told me the *truth* about what was involved. I sometimes think that's why I keep so busy. I'm running away from it, even now. I feel I've got to put something back into the pot to compensate for what I did – hence all my do-gooding.'

She stubbed out her cigarette and stared at the kitchen window.

'I've talked to dozens of women at the Refuge, and I can't get over how often it comes up. And then there was Valda. You remember Valda – the suicide? She'd got it really bad; she had a lot of problems. She'd had two terminations in the last eight months. The last was one of those late abortions where you go through the whole damned labour and see your dead baby. That tipped her over the brink, and I'm not surprised.'

Chloe didn't know what to say, but she and her mother were looking at each other in such a way that you could tell they were understanding each other deep, deep down.

'Why don't you campaign against it, then?' Clo asked at last.

'Because I see some of the awful backgrounds these women are coming from, how desperate they are. They feel they've got no choice because there's no-one there to support them or counsel them if they want to have the kid.'

Another cigarette came out and was lit shakily. She inhaled deeply.

'Even now, I'm not being straight with you,' she said. 'I don't campaign, because I can't admit what I did – *that's* the real reason. I make excuses not to go with Karen and

Sandra on their pro-choice rallies, but I've never told them why. It *haunts* me, Clo – I can't face the implications.

'There's no release from it, no-one to forgive me. I'm telling you now because I think I'd have cracked up – I'm serious – if you'd gone and had an abortion without telling me.'

Clo was blinking hard.

'When I had you,' Mrs P went on, 'I thought it would wipe it away and make everything right. But you can't escape. At every antenatal appointment, they'd ask, "Any previous pregnancies?" and they'd be turning the knife in the wound.

'Even worse was when every moment of every day I watched you grow, cut your teeth, smile, take your first steps and all that . . . you know? It just made the pain deeper. Worse. Made it more real and truer what had happened, who I'd killed. Made me too neurotic for your father to live with.

'All I want is to be able to say I'm sorry. To my son. Oh, God!' she burst out, and buried her face in her hands.

What can you say? Chloe moved across to her mother's side and put her arm around her. I looked at Chloe, so slim in her jeans – nothing showing, *yet*. It *still* seemed unreal that inside her there could be a tiny baby as long as a finger, kicking, smiling and doing somersaults and already equipped with miniature fingers, toes, nerves and a full set of human rights.

I slipped out quietly. They didn't notice.

13

Future . . . perfect?

Tuesday

This morning a parcel arrived from Claude, postmarked Aix-en-Provence and covered in pretty stamps. Inside was a letter for me taped to a small box of *calissons* – marzipan sweets – to thank us for her 'fun time'. Which was nice of her, as she'd already bought my mum a huge plant when she'd left.

There was also a note with instructions for me to pass it on to 'Robint, with the cute butt'. Which left me completely nonplussed; did she mean Robin – or Robert? Neither of whose butts could be described as 'cute' with the wildest leap of the imagination.

Perhaps, I reasoned, if I read it there'd be some clue as to who she meant. But no . . . that wouldn't be *le fair play*. Then again, what the heck?

Nothing from Chloe. Again. I do think she could take time out to drop me a letter. A card, even. I know she's bound to be busy, but it only takes five minutes. Next time, I'll send her that card from Bates' with all the letters of the alphabet except the third, and the caption 'Long time

– no C'.

I miss her. She said I could go over to Morton Green to see her once she'd settled, but I don't know how I feel about that. It might sound silly, but what I can't face is the thought of her in a maternity dress – not that she's probably wearing one yet. I couldn't cope with it. In some ways I'd feel more comfortable keeping things to letters and phone-calls.

Before she went, Clo said, 'Pop in on Hattie from time to time, will you? Keep an eye on her, OK?'

But I haven't – yet. I'd feel embarrassed to go around. I feel so sorry for the woman; sorry that I just wrote her off as nutty when all the time she'd had some bad knocks in life that she couldn't get over. And awkward that I know something about her I feel I haven't got the right to know. You never can tell with people.

The worst of it is the lying.

'Where's Clo?' Cass asked me on the first day of term.

I'd been worrying about what to say. Should I invent some mystery illness? Or pretend she'd met someone and run off to California? In the end, I concocted this tale of her being offered a chance to do graphic design somewhere else that she'd have been mad not to take. That she was staying with relatives.

'Shame about that,' Cass had said, 'because I heard that Toby fancied her.'

How childish.

Jane Soper wouldn't give up on it. 'Graphic design – where?' she insisted.

I blustered a bit.

'So, what A-levels is she doing?'

The girl was relentless. One thing that made it easier was that Clo wasn't the only person who hadn't come back after the summer. Yasmin never returned.

Yazz had had great difficulty persuading her father to let her stay on in the first place, and during the holidays he'd changed his mind and said that it was a waste over-educating a woman. Cass had heard that he'd arranged a marriage for her. We didn't know what to think, really; we wondered how Yazz was taking it.

We never *did* find out, because hers wasn't the sort of home you could drop in on.

And there was the usual smattering of kids you thought you'd seen the last of, but who'd failed their GCSEs and were staying on for the retakes. So perhaps Chloe's absence didn't show as much as I'd feared.

After she went, I told Mum. Everything. I had to. I couldn't bottle it in for ever, and I had to confide in someone. Anyway, Mum knew something was up, and I couldn't lie to her. She was really good about it; she let me cry on her shoulder for ages, just like when I was little.

At least I know Chloe's with a nice crowd. I was determined to resent them, but I couldn't. Donald and Bron invited Clo and her mum around for a meal to iron out the arrangements, and Clo asked if I could go, too. Just like that.

'No,' I said when she told me. 'You can't be *serious!* This is going to be even less enjoyable than a wet week in Dyfed.'

But I already told you I'm a lousy judge. I was as tense as anything as we rang the bell; no matter how nice they were, I was going to hate them on sight.

'Chloe, how lovely to see you! And this must be your mother . . . and Sophie. You're very, very welcome. Come on in,' Donald had said, ushering us into his massive, jumbly hallway. He beamed me a smile that seemed to say, 'I know just what you're thinking and it doesn't matter a bit.'

It was very difficult maintaining my ice-cool in the face of all this *bonhomie*. Mrs P was uptight, too, trying to fathom out what Chloe had got into. And as for Clo – well, she was desperate for us to like the Wilcoxes. And, despite myself, I did.

It was partly the fact that Donald and Bron were genuinely interested in people. I'd gone there expecting to be a spare part, a wallflower – about as much fun as a wet sock on a picnic. And I came away feeling as if I'd been the centre of attention, that my life and hopes and self were of riveting interest.

Bron was one of those people who, after a mere glimpse of Chloe, rushed for their file-index of mail-order recipe cards. Dinner meant Dinner with a capital D. And it was:

For starters, individual puffy cheesy things ('*Gougères*,' said Bron), followed by what looked like leather wallets stuffed with gerbil mix ('*Taboulleh* in pitta,' said Bron). For dessert, there was mango *brûlée* with Greek yoghurt ('Dead easy, really,' said Bron). It all looked weird, but it tasted great.

Sometimes I'd wonder why it wasn't enough just *being* Chloe's friend. Why should I have to *eat* like her, too?

'Tennis, eh?' said Bron enthusiastically over her side-salad. 'I used to play tennis for Sussex when I was your age. I wish I could have got to Wimbledon this year, but it's difficult with the kids. Did you see the ladies' quarter-finals?'

'See it? I was *there*.'

'You weren't! How *fantastic!* Tell me all.'

Unerringly, Bron had homed straight in on the one subject I could happily witter on about for hours, and we ended up having such a fascinating discussion that I forgot

I was supposed to hate the woman.

'So, if you were on the summer tennis school, you probably met Oliver Wedloe. He's a coach there,' Bron continued.

Hadn't I *just*.

'He's a youth leader in our church.'

Mr *Gorgeous-legs*? He never struck me as the religious type.

'You should come along some time – you'd enjoy it. It's very lively.'

Sure – they're probably stuck in a 1960s time-warp singing top hits like *Kumbayah* and *Lord of the Dance* like at our school assemblies, and thinking how cool they are.

'OK,' I said.

No chance. I'd sooner stay in and watch *Highway* with Harry Secombe.

'Oliver's arranged a rock concert next month with a Christian heavy metal band called Swordsman. Come along.'

This intrigued me – I couldn't visualise the felt-hat and bunion brigade bopping to *that*. I might just go, it I could find someone to go with. I'd be at a loose end by then.

And that was another thing. Every conversation led back to the fact that Chloe was going. *Ouch*. I glanced across the table to where Donald was thrashing out practicalities with a slightly-frowning Mrs P, and unexpectedly caught Chloe's eye. She gave me a smile, all teeth and gums, and I grinned back weakly.

'I'm sure I know you from somewhere,' Bron was saying, thinking about it. Then she dredged it out from her grey cells, and her face cleared. 'You babysit for Ruth Gibbs, don't you?'

I was astounded. What was the woman – a mind-reader?

'You know Ruth?'

I wondered how. Ruth and Tony were golf-club-goers, not churchgoers. Not in a month of Sundays. Or Christmas Days or Easter Days.

'Yeah, she's a good friend. I don't see so much of her now she's got the twins, though. We both adopted children at about the same time. I thought I'd heard the names Sophie and Chloe mentioned together somewhere!' Bron finished up, triumphantly.

'Your kids are adopted, too, are they?' I asked.

'Yes . . . and no,' she replied. 'We've got three of our own: Tom, who's nineteen; Julie, who's your age;' (I was beginning to regret having asked) 'and Sebastian, who's nine. Then we adopted Rachel three years ago. She's five. She's Downs – you know, a mongol.'

'Oh,' I said, blushing to the roots of my hair and staring at my *taboulleh*. Trust me to put my foot in it.

'She's a delight, a pure delight,' Bron went on. 'Hard work, I grant you, but I'd never be without her. Look at that picture over there.'

She gestured at a psychedelic splodge Blu-tacked to the wall.

'She did that at school today. Fantastic, isn't it?'

Well, it would have been churlish to disagree.

'That's partly why we're so involved with The Haven,' said Bron, breaking off a chunk of French bread and offering it to me. 'Kids like that are routinely aborted these days. Come over some time – she'd love to meet you. She enjoys new friends.'

'Thanks,' I mumbled.

Bron launched into her curly, red lettuce ('*Lollo rosso*,' she said it was called). Donald and Mrs P were talking about financial arrangements at the other end of the table, and I stared around, still trying to get the measure of the people who were going to take my friend away.

In Donald and Bron I recognised that same something that had come over Chloe, and for some reason it made me feel lonely. It was unnerving. I felt as if they possessed something that I didn't have and that I needed. Despite myself, I found it compulsive and I was curious to know more. Not that I was going to *admit* it, of course.

'Chloe's going to be leaving on Friday,' Bron said, gently. 'They're arranging it now. It might be a very long weekend for you; we're having a fellowship picnic on Sunday straight after the meeting, so why don't you come? I *mean* it. This is a genuine invitation, Sophie.'

'Oh, I don't know,' I said, caught off-guard and feeling confused. 'I won't know anyone. I haven't got transport, anyway. It's very kind and everything, but I'll probably want to be on my own.'

'Think about it,' said Bron. 'Here's my number. If you change your mind, just ring.'

I never did, but I should have. All day Sunday I was depressed and bored out of my mind, wishing I'd gone and feeling bad that I hadn't. I should have taken Chloe's advice.

'They mean it, you know,' she'd said, stuffing things into her suitcase. 'If they invite you, they aren't just *saying* it. Not like some people. They're a really nice family.'

'Aha! Your secret's out! So, what's Tom like?'

'Tom? Now, *there's* a guy you could really trust,' Clo said thoughtfully. There was something about the way she said it that made me wonder. Just for a moment.

'Before you fill up all the space in your case, I'll give you this,' I said, embarrassed, handing her the going-away present I'd bought her. It was a selection of watercolour tubes in a wooden case. I don't know the first thing about art, and they had taken about four weeks' wages from Bates'. She'd better like them.

'I kept the receipt in case you want to change it,' I said anxiously.

'Change it? Oh, Sophie, you nut – it's *perfect!* That's the set I've always promised myself. How did you know?'

'Just a lucky guess,' I admitted, pleased that *she* was pleased.

'I'll send you some paintings of my new place,' Clo said.

'And I'll keep them in case I can make a few quid out of them when you're famous,' I joked.

'Yeah,' she said, and silence fell.

She was keeping pretty cool in the circumstances. I was afraid that her religious experience was going to suddenly pop and leave her flat, and I kept waiting for it to happen. But it didn't.

I *know* she was scared and apprehensive and wished she wasn't going. She told me. But she also said she felt peaceful inside about it, that she knew it was the right thing to do and that everything was going to be OK. There was something so *different*, so assertive about her these days that you just couldn't argue.

I was genuinely glad she'd found a crutch to help her through what was coming. Boy, she'd need it.

'It's *not* a crutch, Sophie. It's real! Try it and see.'

But that didn't make me feel any better. It was still all Martian to me.

Now that it was nearly time for her to go, we were feeling the strain of it. We didn't want the crucial moment to come, but in some ways we wished it would, because the suspense was killing us. We kept running out of things to say. So we ended up saying stupid things.

'So, you *will* write?' I asked.

'Of *course.* And you'll come and visit me?'

'Of *course,*' I mimicked. And the thought of it churned up all my emotions again.

'You've got John and Fiona's address?' she asked.

I nodded.

'Oh, Sophie!' she bleated, and then she started to cry. That started me off again. I blinked furiously and stared frantically out of the window.

'Oh, Clo – you silly cow!' I said, sniffing. 'Whatever did you have to go and get pregnant for?'

* * *

Wednesday

There was a letter on the mat for me this morning. Morton Green postmark. This was from Chloe. Definitely. I tore it open and went back to my room to read it in private.

It was a wonder she'd fitted it in the envelope – she'd scrawled it on at least eight sheets of airmail-type paper with about four different-coloured pens. Page one was a week old.

I always read things from the back, so I turned to the last sheet; yesterday's date.

> I'm settling in nicely. John and Fiona have been very kind to me. Fi's really mumsy, good-in-a-crisis, easy to talk to, that sort of thing. Reminds we a bit of your mum. Personality-wise, *not* the hairstyle! And she's veggie. Well, a demi-veg.

What was a demi-veg? Someone who ate half a hamburger?

I asked her if it was OK for you to come and stay one weekend, and she said that was fine; her son lives in Newley – must be near you – and he comes over once a month. She said she could ask him to give you a lift. He sounds really nice – your type. Looks fanciable from the photos. His name's Oliver and he's a sports teacher.

John and Fiona Wedloe. She didn't tell me they were called John and Fiona *Wedloe!*

Shall I put in a good word for you, nudge, nudge, wink, wink?!

Yes, yes . . . most *definitely.*

It's really nice here, and the college is going to work out great. I'm getting to know people now. What did the girls say about me disappearing? Everybody's being really kind here, but I miss you all like crazy. I miss Hattie. I really do. Have you been round to see her like I told you? Well, *get on* with it!

Why haven't you written, Sophie? You can be really lazy without me around to keep an eye on you. I'd be glad of some mail – I'd get more of a reaction from Puddy Tat.

I can't do my jeans up anymore. I'm going for a scan next week – that's like a kind of X-ray to check that the baby's OK.

Please say you'll come and stay. Please, please, please, PLEASE!

Lotsalove, etc,

Chloe

I started to mentally compose my reply. Nothing *too* obvious, you understand. Dead cool, that's me.

Dear Clo,

Why don't you write shorter and oftener 'cos you don't let me get a word in edgeways. Yes, I'd love to come. Tell Mrs Wedloe to give Oliver my phone number and he can ring to arrange a lift. Tell him I'd also love a ticket for his rock concert.

Definitely.

After reading this book, you may want further help and advice on pregnancy and pro-life issues. If so, contact one or more of the following organisations:

Care
53 Romney Street
London SW1P 3RF
Tel: 071-233 0455

LIFE
LIFE House
Newbold Terrace
Leamington Spa CV32 4EA
Tel: 0926-421587

SPUC
7 Tufton Street
Westminster
London SW1P 3QN
Tel: 071-222 5845

Christians Caring for Life
107 Firgrove Road
Southampton SO1 3ET
Tel: 0703-783134

Also in Harvestime's **Life Choices** series:

Blind Spot
by Liz Priestley

I pulled a face as the front door shut behind my sister, Karen, sending a strong whiff of perfume eddying through the hall.

I hate the way she destroys a bit more of the ozone layer every time she sprays her skin.

'You do for ecology what Big Daddy does for hang-gliding,' I told her the other day.

I hate her, and do my best to score off her whenever my parents are out. She can't even take a little joke at her expense!

Auntie Jean raised the subject when I was around at her place. 'How are we going to deal with this blind spot, Sandy?' she asked me.

'What blind spot? I haven't got a blind spot!'

'You see the danger immediately when it comes to the destruction of the rain forest; can't you see that the same principles apply to people, too? You've been systematically destroying your sister's self-esteem to pump up your own pride.'

After that remark, I've decided I'm never going round to Auntie Jean's again.

ISBN 0-947714-97-9

£2.95

Also in Harvestime's **Life Choices** series:

Over the Edge
by Audrey Constant

When Terry mysteriously plunges to his death over the cliff, Jo's tranquil world is shattered for ever.

Soon she finds herself involved in helping another speedway enthusiast – Danny – who has lost interest in life because of his best friend's tragic death-wish.

Danny's behaviour, like Terry's, is a mystery. He is erratic on the speedway track and subject to swings of mood.

Jo goes with Danny to join in a 'game' in which Terry is supposed to speak to them from beyond the grave. She is so terrified by the experience that she switches on the lights and abruptly breaks the spell.

Will Danny join Terry in a death-wish plunge over the cliff? Will Jo be able to convince Danny of the dangers of occult involvement?

Is there any way to break the hold the spirit world seems to have on Danny's life?

ISBN 0-947714-98-7

£2.95